the $10
Gourmet

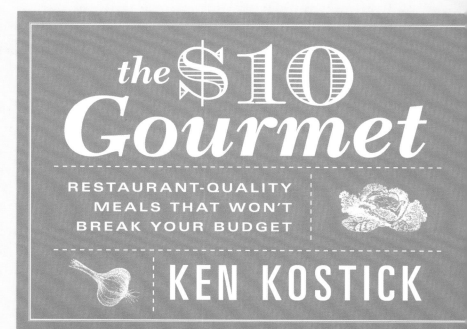

the $10 Gourmet

RESTAURANT-QUALITY MEALS THAT WON'T BREAK YOUR BUDGET

KEN KOSTICK

whitecap

Whitecap Books is known for its expertise in
the cookbook market, and has produced some
of the most innovative and familiar titles found
in kitchens across North America. Visit our
website at www.whitecap.ca.

EDITING   Melva McLean
PROOFREADING   Lesley Cameron
COVER & INTERIOR DESIGN   Mauve Pagé
FOOD PHOTOGRAPHY   Bobb Barratt
FOOD STYLING   Tanya Scata

PRINTED IN CANADA BY FRIESENS

LIBRARY AND ARCHIVES CANADA
CATALOGUING IN PUBLICATION

Kostick, Ken, 1954–
   The $10 gourmet / Ken Kostick.

ISBN 978-1-77050-005-1

   1. Low budget cookery. 2. Quick and easy
cookery. I. Title. II. Title: Ten dollar gourmet.

TX652.K68 2009   641.5'52
C2009-902675-9

The publisher acknowledges the financial
support of the Government of Canada through
the Canada Book Fund (CBF) and the Province
of British Columbia through the Book Publish-
ing Tax Credit.

09 10 11 12 13   5 4 3 2 1

CONTENTS

In these difficult economic times we are all looking for ways to save money on meals without compromising taste and quality. This cookbook shows you how to make restaurant-quality main meals for two for under $10! If you enjoy Mediterranean stuffed chicken, shrimp penne, or a spicy Asian beef stir-fry, you don't have to wait until you have enough money to go out. You can make these dishes at home in three easy steps and always under $10.

One of the keys to making economical meals quickly is to keep essential ingredients on hand in your pantry and in your refrigerator. Expensive, you ask? Not really. You can get your essential pantry and refrigerator items for under $50 (see pages xi and xii). Once you have your essential items on hand, check out each recipe's shopping list for the additional ingredients you'll need. Economical restaurant-quality meals also start with smart and effective shopping habits. I have a few, which I share with you on the following pages. From soups to sauces I will show you how to stretch your grocery dollar. By using scraps from asparagus, broccoli, mushroom stems, and any vegetable you would normally take the ends off and throw out, you can make incredible soups and even sauces for your main meals.

Avoid buying pre-made or frozen meals because the price includes the convenience of having someone else do the labour. You can actually make most of these meals yourself and for much less money. If you have limited time to cook dinner, prepare some of the restaurant-quality dishes in this book and freeze them to enjoy at a later date.

But what about entertaining, you might wonder. No problem. Check out pages 158 to 169 for three fantastic menus that serve 6 people for under $30.

I enjoy the creative challenge of preparing recipes that are not only economical but also easy to prepare and healthy. When you grocery shop, look for non- or low-fat items. You can find low-fat stocks, cheeses, yogurt, coconut milk, and sour cream. In addition, using grapeseed oil instead of regular vegetable oil cuts down on the fat count.

Enjoy saving money without sacrificing good taste.

Bon appétit!
Ken

SMART &
EFFECTIVE SHOPPING

Don't do what I used to do—walk up and down every aisle in the nearest grocery store and just buy what you need. It won't save you money! While researching *The $10 Gourmet*, I found I really needed to educate myself about smart and effective shopping. And when I did, I was surprised at how poor my shopping skills really were!

Do your research and change your habits. It's not always easy, but you'll be surprised at what a big difference a few simple things will make to your grocery budget. The following are tips I want to share with you, to help you shop smart too. The prices in this book aren't always average prices (and prices will naturally vary according to region), but they reflect the actual prices I paid after applying these smart shopping strategies.

EAT BEFORE YOU SHOP. Do not shop hungry! If you are like me, you will tend to buy more than you need when hungry. Eat a snack before shopping.

WRITE IT DOWN. While doing research for this book, I kept a spreadsheet. If you're committed to saving money, writing things down will help you to recognize a bargain when you see it.

SHOP AT DIFFERENT STORES. This is a must if you want to really save. For example, I found a couple of stores that had great prices on produce but not on non-perishables. Some stores specialize in meats and frozen items. You don't have to visit both on the same day. I buy produce at one place, meat at another, and then non-perishables somewhere else. I know I can always find at least one or two deals at any store, and I stick to those deals.

SHOPPING LIST. Always use a shopping list. Each recipe in *The $10 Gourmet* includes a shopping list in the form of a receipt that you can use to add to your regular shopping list. Only purchase items on your list; try not to deviate.

COUPONS. Yes, coupons! When you enter a supermarket, stop and pick up their flyer and see if they have coupons for any of the items on your list.

READ THE FLYERS. It doesn't take a lot of time to browse a flyer. If you don't have flyers delivered to your house or apartment, check out the websites of your local stores where you can often browse flyers online. This is where you'll find the best deals.

NO-NAME/GENERIC PRODUCTS. Do not be afraid of no-name or generic products. I did a comparison of some regular brand items with no-name or generic brands of similar quality. The brand items cost a total of $118.46, while the no-name items cost $83.22; that's an overall savings of $35.24 for the same quality. Can you imagine how much you can save in a year just by buying generic?

BUY IN BULK. There are a few key items that are great to buy in bulk—canned goods, for example, are often much cheaper when you buy them by the case. Also be willing to buy large quantities of meat when you find it on sale and freeze it. You'll find that when it comes to stocking your pantry, you'll save more in the long run by spending a little more up front.

CHECK THE END-CAP DISPLAYS. Always check out the end-caps, the displays at the ends of aisles. A supermarket will display its best-valued items at the end-caps so that you are less likely to miss them.

SCHEDULE YOUR SHOPPING TIME. Whenever I have time to spare, I know that I am more likely to look around and spend more money. Plan in advance to limit the time you are going to spend at the supermarket. Schedule your visit with just enough time to find your items and check out. The less time you have available to browse and shop, the less you will spend.

YOUR KITCHEN & MONEY-SAVING TIPS

Along with smart and effective shopping at your local supermarkets, you can find other ways to save a lot of money—namely, reducing waste. The average household wastes an estimated one-third of its weekly groceries. That's like throwing cash in the garbage! Don't let it happen to you.

INVEST IN A GOOD BONING KNIFE

Learn to bone and skin poultry yourself. Avoid paying more for meat that has already been prepared for you.

FREEZE VEGETABLE ENDS

Use a large freezer bag to store vegetable ends that you would normally throw out—asparagus, broccoli, cauliflower, celery, mushrooms, red and green peppers, and tomatoes. After a couple of weeks, you'll have enough vegetable ends to make a fantastic sauce or soup.

DRY FRESH HERBS

How often do you buy fresh bunches of herbs, use some for one meal, and let the rest go to waste? We all do that. The solution is to use what you need, then place (or hang) what remains of the bunch in a warm, dry, well-ventilated area. In a couple of days, the herbs will be dry, and you can crush and place them in a container. You can make 3 to 4 ounces (about 125 g) of dried herbs out of one large bunch of fresh, an amount that costs about $0.99 to buy.

MAKE YOUR OWN SAUCES, MARINADES & SALAD DRESSINGS

Store-bought salad dressings can cost $3.00 to $6.00 a bottle, but you can make a salad dressing that has a lot of flavour for less than $1.00. I've given you some great recipes in this book, but the general ratio when making your own dressing is two-thirds oil to one-third vinegar. For marinades it's one-third oil to two-thirds of juice, like orange or apple. Add herbs and spices for flavour as well as fresh garlic and onion. Just remember that if you use fresh ingredients like garlic or onion you must use the salad dressing within a week.

ROAST YOUR OWN GARLIC

Roasted garlic is a wonderful addition to your refrigerator. Peel the garlic cloves and brush them with olive oil. Roast them on a cooking sheet in an oven at 350°F (180°C) for about 10 to 15 minutes, or until golden. Allow them to cool and dry slightly, chop them up, and store in a container in the refrigerator for up to a week.

ESSENTIAL PANTRY ITEMS FOR LESS THAN $50

....

I believe that there are essential items you need in your pantry to prepare really flavourful and healthy meals. The one thing you do not need to do is spend a lot of money. Smart and effective shopping is the key. You can do what I do and visit different local supermarkets to get the best prices.

> If you keep your pantry and refrigerator stocked, you should only need to pick up a few fresh ingredients to make all of the recipes in this book. See the shopping lists on each page.

PANTRY ITEM	AMOUNT	PRICE
Balsamic vinegar	2 cups (500 mL)	$ 2.19
Beef bouillon	6 cubes	$ 0.99
Brown sugar	5 oz (150 g)	$ 1.29
Cayenne pepper	4 oz (125 g)	$ 0.99
Chicken bouillon	6 cubes	$ 0.99
Chili powder	4 oz (125 g)	$ 0.99
Cinnamon	4 oz (125 g)	$ 0.99
Coconut milk	5½ oz (156 mL)	$ 0.77
Cumin seed	4 oz (125 g)	$ 1.47
Cooking wine—red	2 cups (500 mL)	$ 1.49
Cooking wine—white	2 cups (500 mL)	$ 1.49
Curry powder	4 oz (125 g)	$ 0.99
Dried basil	4 oz (125 g)	$ 0.99
Dried cilantro	4 oz (125 g)	$ 0.99
Dried dill	4 oz (125 g)	$ 0.99
Dried mint	4 oz (125 g)	$ 0.99
Dried oregano	4 oz (125 g)	$ 0.99
Dried parsley	4 oz (125 g)	$ 0.99
Dried rosemary	4 oz (125 g)	$ 0.99
Dried tarragon	4 oz (125 g)	$ 0.99
Dried thyme	4 oz (125 g)	$ 0.99
Garlic powder	4 oz (125 g)	$ 0.89
Liquid honey	½ lb (250 g)	$ 2.10
Olive oil	2 cups (500 mL)	$ 4.97
Onion powder	4 oz (125 g)	$ 0.89
Red pepper flakes	4 oz (125 g)	$ 0.99
Panko breadcrumbs	2½ cups (750 mL)	$ 1.83
Red wine vinegar	2 cups (500 mL)	$ 1.29
Saffron threads	1 oz (32 g)	$ 2.99
Sesame oil	¾ cup (185 mL)	$ 2.39
Soy sauce	1¾ cups (435 mL)	$ 1.17
Sugar	5 oz (150 g)	$ 1.29
Vegetable bouillon	6 cubes	$ 0.99
Wasabi paste	1 oz (41 g)	$ 1.49
White wine vinegar	2 cups (500 mL)	$ 1.10
TOTAL		**$ 47.93**

ESSENTIAL REFRIGERATOR ITEMS FOR LESS THAN $50

....

An economical kitchen requires a fully stocked refrigerator. I like to have the products listed below on hand to prepare meals that are easy to make and don't cost a lot. These products are usually produced by a handful of national companies and will vary in price from one supermarket to another. When purchasing any item with an expiry date, reach towards the back of the displays, where they stock items with longer expiry dates.

While researching for this book, I carefully recorded each item that I purchased. As a result, you might find two slightly different prices for the same item in two different recipes. That's because I may have found a bunch of asparagus at one store one day for $2.99 (great price!), but then found a bunch of asparagus at another store for $2.76 (even better). The prices fluctuate from place to place, and week to week, but you can always find a great price if you shop carefully.

REFRIGERATOR ITEM	AMOUNT	PRICE
Apple juice	5 cups (1.25 L)	$ 1.49
Applesauce	1 cup (250 mL)	$ 1.69
Butter	1 lb (454 g)	$ 3.09
Cranberry juice	4 cups (1 L)	$ 2.99
Dijon mustard	1½ cups (375 mL)	$ 1.89
Extra large eggs	1 dozen	$ 1.79
Hoisin sauce	1¾ cups (455 mL)	$ 1.70
Homo milk	4 cups (1 L)	$ 2.69
Light cream (10%)	2-cup carton (500 mL)	$ 2.79
Orange juice	4 cups (1 L)	$ 2.99
Pear nectar	4 cups (1 L)	$ 3.49
Skim milk	4 cups (1 L)	$ 1.89
Sour cream	2 cups (500 mL)	$ 2.59
	1 cup (250 mL)	$ 1.89
Whipping cream (35%)	2 cups (500 mL)	$ 2.89
	1 cup (250 mL)	$ 1.89
Worcestershire sauce	10 fl oz (284 mL) bottle	$ 1.49
Yogurt, plain	2-cup container (300 mL)	$ 2.49
TOTAL		$ 41.73

SOUPS & STEWS

CAULIFLOWER SOUP WITH BLUE CHEESE

The combination of cauliflower and blue cheese
makes this a hearty soup with lots of deep flavour. SERVES 2

INGREDIENTS

3 Tbsp (45 mL) olive oil

1 small red onion, chopped

2 cloves garlic, chopped

4 cups (1 L) cauliflower florets

4 cups (1 L) vegetable stock

½ tsp (2 mL) dried thyme

½ tsp (2 mL) dried basil

½ tsp (2 mL) sea salt

½ tsp (2 mL) ground black pepper

1 cup (250 mL) light cream or whipping cream

½ cup (125 mL) crumbled blue cheese

1 apple, thinly sliced (optional)

METHOD

1. Heat the oil in a medium-sized pot. Sauté the onion and garlic for 3–4 minutes, or until the onions are translucent.

2. Add all the other ingredients, except the cream, blue cheese, and apple. Bring to a boil then reduce the heat and simmer for 15 minutes.

3. Using a hand blender, purée the soup until smooth. Gently stir in the cream and blue cheese. Garnish with apple slices, if using.

SHOPPING LIST

RED ONION	$0.33
GARLIC	$0.07
CAULIFLOWER	$2.61
BLUE CHEESE	$3.39
APPLE	$0.47
TOTAL	$6.87

EASY CRABMEAT BISQUE WITH WHITE WINE & SALSA

The nip of salsa in this crabmeat bisque gives it that added edge. It's just as good with shrimp instead of crabmeat. SERVES 2

INGREDIENTS

4 cups (1 L) vegetable or
fish stock

one 14 oz (398 mL) can
diced tomatoes

1 cup (250 mL) canned
crabmeat, drained

½ cup (125 mL) white
cooking wine

½ cup (125 mL) mild salsa

1 small onion, chopped

2 cloves garlic, chopped

2 Tbsp (30 mL) balsamic
vinegar

1 tsp (5 mL) chili powder

½ tsp (2 mL) dried basil

½ tsp (2 mL) dried thyme

½ tsp (2 mL) sea salt

½ tsp (2 mL) ground black
pepper

½ cup (125 mL) light cream
or whipping cream

METHOD

1. Combine all of the ingredients, except the cream, in a large pot. Bring to a boil then reduce the heat. Simmer for 15 minutes.
2. Using a hand blender, purée the soup until smooth.
3. Add the whipping cream and stir gently.

```
          SHOPPING LIST
       -----------------------

CANNED TOMATOES        $0.87
CRABMEAT               $5.06
SALSA                  $2.99
ONION                  $0.13
GARLIC                 $0.07
       =======================
TOTAL                  $9.12
```

CHICKEN STEW WITH RED WINE & SAGE

*Stretch your food dollar by using leftover chicken and vegetables to make this stew.
You can replace the diced chicken with diced turkey or four chopped portobello mushrooms.* SERVES 2

INGREDIENTS

2 Tbsp (30 mL) olive oil

2 chicken breasts, skinned, boned, and diced

2 cloves garlic, chopped

1 small red onion, chopped

1 green bell pepper, chopped

½ cup (125 mL) red cooking wine

2 potatoes, cubed

4 cups (1 L) chicken stock

one 14 oz (398 mL) can diced tomatoes

1 tsp (5 mL) dried sage

½ tsp (2 mL) dried basil

½ tsp (2 mL) sea salt

½ tsp (2 mL) ground black pepper

METHOD

1. Heat the oil in a medium-sized pot. Brown the diced chicken for 4–5 minutes. Add the garlic, red onion, and green bell pepper and sauté for another 4–5 minutes.

2. Add the red cooking wine and allow it to reduce for 3–4 minutes. Add all of the remaining ingredients. Bring to a boil then reduce the heat. Simmer for about 15 minutes.

SHOPPING LIST

CHICKEN BREASTS	$4.37
GARLIC	$0.07
RED ONION	$0.33
GREEN BELL PEPPER	$0.76
POTATOES	$0.72
CANNED TOMATOES	$0.87
TOTAL	$7.12

RED PEPPER SOUP WITH SUN-DRIED TOMATOES & SWISS CHEESE

Red pepper is an especially flavourful vegetable and it makes an excellent cream soup, very hearty and filling. SERVES 2

INGREDIENTS

2 Tbsp (30 mL) olive oil

1 small onion, chopped

2 cloves garlic, chopped

3 large red bell peppers, chopped

4 cups (1 L) vegetable stock

¼ cup (60 mL) chopped sun-dried tomatoes

½ tsp (2 mL) dried basil

½ tsp (2 mL) sea salt

½ tsp (2 mL) ground black pepper

¼ cup (60 mL) light cream or whipping cream

2 slices Swiss cheese, chopped

METHOD

1. Heat the oil in a medium-sized pot. Sauté the onion, garlic, and red bell pepper for 5–6 minutes, or until the peppers are tender.
2. Add all of the remaining ingredients, except the cream and Swiss cheese. Bring to a boil then reduce the heat. Simmer for 10–12 minutes.
3. Using a hand blender, purée the soup until nice and smooth. Gently stir in the cream and Swiss cheese.

SHOPPING LIST

ONION	$0.13
GARLIC	$0.07
RED BELL PEPPERS	$4.68
SUN-DRIED TOMATOES	$1.35
SWISS CHEESE	$1.60
TOTAL	$7.83

TURKEY & WHITE BEAN CHILI

*Wow! You will love this recipe. It's light but actually fills you up. Add 2 cups (500 mL)
of stock and you have a great soup for four people (pictured). You can replace the ground turkey
with ground chicken or ground beef. For a vegetarian option, use 4 cups (1 L)
chopped mushrooms and vegetable stock.* SERVES 2

INGREDIENTS

2 Tbsp (30 mL) olive oil

1 lb (500 g) lean ground turkey

1 small onion, chopped

2 celery stalks, chopped

1 small green bell pepper, chopped

one 28 oz (796 mL) can diced tomatoes

1 cup (250 mL) cooked or canned white kidney beans

½ cup (125 mL) chicken stock, more if needed

½ cup (125 mL) kernel corn, frozen or canned

2 Tbsp (30 mL) liquid honey

½ tsp (2 mL) dried basil

½ tsp (2 mL) dried oregano

½ tsp (2 mL) chili powder

½ tsp (2 mL) sea salt

½ tsp (2 mL) ground black pepper

METHOD

1. Heat the olive oil in a medium-sized pot. Sauté the ground turkey until cooked.

2. Add the onion, celery, and green pepper, and sauté for 4–5 minutes, or until the vegetables are translucent.

3. Add all of the remaining ingredients and simmer on low for 15 minutes. Add more stock if it's too thick.

SHOPPING LIST

GROUND TURKEY	$3.33
ONION	$0.13
CELERY	$1.67
GREEN BELL PEPPER	$0.51
CANNED TOMATOES	$1.24
WHITE KIDNEY BEANS	$0.78
CORN	$0.89
TOTAL	**$8.55**

HEARTY FALL STEW WITH RED WINE & DIJON

This beef stew offers a comfort-food meal with a lot of flavour and low cost. You can use cubed chicken, turkey, or pork instead of beef. For a vegetarian option, replace the beef with 4 cups (1 L) mushrooms and use vegetable stock instead of beef stock. SERVES 2

INGREDIENTS

- 2 Tbsp (30 mL) olive oil
- 1 lb (500 g) stewing beef, cubed
- 1 carrot, peeled and chopped
- 1 small onion, chopped
- 2 cloves garlic, chopped
- 1 green bell pepper, chopped
- 2 celery stalks, chopped
- ½ cup (125 mL) cooking red wine
- 3 cups (750 mL) beef stock
- 2 potatoes, peeled and cubed
- 2 Tbsp (30 mL) Dijon mustard
- 2 Tbsp (30 mL) Worcestershire sauce
- ½ tsp (2 mL) dried basil
- ½ tsp (2 mL) dried thyme
- ½ tsp (2 mL) sea salt
- ½ tsp (2 mL) ground black pepper

METHOD

1. Heat the oil in a medium-sized pot. Gently sauté the beef on all sides for 3–4 minutes. Add the carrot, onion, garlic, green pepper, and celery. Sauté for another 3–4 minutes.
2. Add the red wine and deglaze the pan, sautéing for another 2–3 minutes.
3. Add all of the remaining ingredients and bring to a boil. Reduce the heat and simmer for 15 minutes. Serve immediately.

SHOPPING LIST

STEWING BEEF	$5.44
CARROT	$0.19
ONION	$0.13
GARLIC	$0.07
GREEN BELL PEPPER	$0.76
CELERY	$1.67
POTATOES	$0.72
TOTAL	**$8.98**

POTATO & LEEK SOUP WITH BACON & DIJON

The combination of potatoes, leeks, and bacon makes this soup burst with flavour. SERVES 2

INGREDIENTS

¼ lb (125 g) bacon, chopped

2 cloves garlic, chopped

2 leeks, cleaned and sliced

4 potatoes, peeled and cubed

1 small red bell pepper, chopped

1 small red onion, chopped

4 cups (1 L) vegetable stock

2 Tbsp (30 mL) balsamic vinegar

2 Tbsp (30 mL) Dijon mustard

½ tsp (2 mL) dried thyme

½ tsp (2 mL) sea salt

½ tsp (2 mL) ground black pepper

½ cup (125 mL) light cream or whipping cream

½ cup (125 mL) chopped fresh parsley

METHOD

1. Cook the bacon in a medium-sized pot for 4–5 minutes, or until brown. Remove the chopped bacon and set aside. Add the garlic and all of the vegetables and continue to sauté for another 4–5 minutes.

2. Add all of the remaining ingredients, except the cream and parsley. Bring to a boil then reduce the heat. Simmer for about 15 minutes.

3. Using a hand blender, purée the soup until smooth. Gently stir in the cream. Stir in the parsley, or use as a garnish. Top with bacon.

SHOPPING LIST

BACON	$2.82
GARLIC	$0.07
LEEKS	$2.69
POTATOES	$1.44
RED BELL PEPPER	$0.96
RED ONION	$0.33
FRESH PARSLEY	$0.99
TOTAL	**$9.30**

HOMEMADE CLAM CHOWDER WITH CHILI POWDER & CHEDDAR

You don't see clam chowder that often on menus but you can make it at home.
It doesn't require too much work or money to prepare. SERVES 2

INGREDIENTS

3 Tbsp (45 mL) olive oil

2 medium potatoes, peeled and cubed

2 celery stalks, chopped

1 carrot, peeled and diced

1 small onion, diced

1 small red bell pepper, diced

4 cups (1 L) vegetable or fish stock

1 cup (250 mL) canned clams, rinsed and drained

1 Tbsp (15 mL) chili powder

½ tsp (2 mL) dried basil

½ tsp (2 mL) dried thyme

½ tsp (2 mL) sea salt

½ tsp (2 mL) ground black pepper

½ cup (125 mL) light cream or whipping cream

½ cup (125 mL) shredded cheddar cheese

METHOD

1. Heat the oil in a medium-sized pot. Sauté all of the vegetables for 6–8 minutes.

2. Add all of the other ingredients, except the cream and cheese. Bring to a boil then reduce the heat. Simmer for about 15 minutes.

3. Add the cream and cheese and stir until smooth.

SHOPPING LIST

POTATOES	$0.72
CELERY	$1.67
CARROT	$0.19
ONION	$0.13
RED BELL PEPPER	$0.96
CANNED CLAMS	$3.98
CHEDDAR CHEESE	$1.90
TOTAL	**$9.55**

SMOKED SALMON SOUP WITH CAPERS & SHALLOTS

Smoked salmon or smoked trout in any recipe will give you a restaurant-quality taste without you ever having to leave home. SERVES 2

INGREDIENTS

2 Tbsp (30 mL) olive oil

4 shallots, diced

1 red bell pepper, diced

½ cup (125 mL) finely chopped smoked salmon

4 cups (1 L) vegetable or fish stock

2 Tbsp (30 mL) capers

½ tsp (2 mL) Dijon mustard

½ tsp (2 mL) chili powder

½ tsp (2 mL) sea salt

½ tsp (2 mL) ground black pepper

½ cup (125 mL) light cream or whipping cream

METHOD

1. Heat the oil in a pot. Sauté the shallots, red bell pepper, and smoked salmon for 4–5 minutes.
2. Add all of the remaining ingredients, except the cream. Bring to a boil then reduce the heat. Simmer for about 15 minutes.
3. Gently stir in the cream.

SHOPPING LIST

SHALLOTS	$1.99
RED BELL PEPPER	$1.56
SMOKED SALMON	$3.99
CAPERS	$2.27
TOTAL	$9.81

BLACK BEAN SOUP WITH CHICKEN & FRESH CORIANDER

Black beans are not only healthy, they're also delicious in soups, stews, and rice dishes. This recipe calls for black beans, but you can use red or white kidney beans instead. SERVES 2

INGREDIENTS

2 Tbsp (30 mL) olive oil

5–6 chicken thighs, skinned, boned, and chopped

1 small red onion, chopped

1 carrot, peeled and diced

2 celery stalks, chopped

1 small red bell pepper, chopped

4 cups (1 L) chicken stock, more if needed

1 cup (250 mL) cooked or canned black beans

1 small tomato, diced

1 Tbsp (15 mL) chili powder

½ tsp (2 mL) dried basil

½ tsp (2 mL) sea salt

½ tsp (2 mL) ground black pepper

½ cup (125 mL) chopped fresh coriander

METHOD

1. Heat the oil in a medium-sized pot. Sauté the chicken for 4–5 minutes. Add the onion, carrot, celery, and red pepper. Sauté for another 4 minutes.

2. Add all of the remaining ingredients, except the coriander. Bring to a boil then reduce the heat. Simmer for 15–20 minutes. If the soup's too thick, add more chicken stock.

3. Add the fresh coriander, mix, and serve.

SHOPPING LIST

CHICKEN THIGHS	$4.54
RED ONION	$0.33
CARROT	$0.19
CELERY	$1.67
RED BELL PEPPER	$0.96
BLACK BEANS	$0.80
TOMATO	$0.51
FRESH CORIANDER	$0.94
TOTAL	$9.94

FISH & SEAFOOD

KENNY'S SPICY CRAB CAKES

Crab cakes are one of my favourite dinnertime meals. I often use finely chopped cooked shrimp in place of the crabmeat. SERVES 2

INGREDIENTS

- 1 cup (250 mL) canned crabmeat, drained
- 1 cup (250 mL) panko breadcrumbs
- 1 small red bell pepper, finely chopped
- 1 small onion, finely chopped
- 1 egg
- 1 Tbsp (15 mL) Dijon mustard
- 1 Tbsp (15 mL) liquid honey
- 1 tsp (5 mL) chili powder
- ½ tsp (2 mL) cayenne pepper
- ½ tsp (2 mL) sea salt
- ½ tsp (2 mL) ground black pepper
- 2 Tbsp (30 mL) olive oil

METHOD

1. Combine all of the ingredients, except the olive oil, in a bowl. Mix well and shape into 4 patties.
2. Heat the olive oil in a sauté pan on medium heat and brown the crab cakes for 15 minutes, turning once.
3. Serve with a nicely flavoured mayonnaise, if desired. Just add some wasabi to the mayonnaise, for example.

SHOPPING LIST

CANNED CRABMEAT	$2.53
RED BELL PEPPER	$0.96
ONION	$0.13
TOTAL	$3.62

GRILLED LEMON SALMON WITH SWEET RED PEPPER PURÉE

This combination is citrusy and fishy but by adding a lovely red pepper purée you end up with a restaurant-quality meal. You can use tuna instead of salmon. To create a vegetarian delight, replace the fish with four large portobello mushrooms. SERVES 2

INGREDIENTS

½ tsp (2 mL) dried basil

½ tsp (2 mL) dried thyme

½ tsp (2 mL) onion powder

¼ cup (60 mL) lemon juice

2 large salmon steaks

1 small red bell pepper, chopped

½ cup (125 mL) apple juice

2 Tbsp (30 mL) balsamic vinegar

1 Tbsp (15 mL) liquid honey

½ tsp (2 mL) sea salt

½ tsp (2 mL) ground black pepper

METHOD

1. Combine the basil, thyme, and onion powder in a small bowl. Sprinkle the lemon juice over the salmon. Coat the salmon with the dried ingredients mixture.
2. Grill the salmon on high heat for 4–5 minutes per side.
3. Combine the remaining ingredients in a blender. Blend or purée until smooth. Serve cold alongside the fish.

SHOPPING LIST

LEMON	$0.33
SALMON STEAKS	$5.80
RED BELL PEPPER	$0.96
TOTAL	$7.09

GARLIC TILAPIA WITH FENNEL & TARRAGON

Tilapia is a nice rich fish abundant in flavour. Years ago it was hard to find, but today it's usually cut into fillets and available in most supermarkets. If you can't find it, just used red snapper instead. SERVES 2

INGREDIENTS

3 Tbsp (45 mL) olive oil

1 small fennel bulb, stalks and outside layer removed, cored, and chopped

1 small onion, chopped

4 cloves garlic, chopped

4 tilapia fillets

½ cup (125 mL) apple juice

2 Tbsp (30 mL) lemon juice

1 tsp (5 mL) dry tarragon

½ tsp (2 mL) sea salt

½ tsp (2 mL) ground black pepper

METHOD

1. Heat the oil in a saucepan. Add the fennel, onion, and garlic and sauté the mixture for 2–3 minutes or until the vegetables are tender. Add the fish. Cook for 3–5 minutes.

2. Mix in all of the remaining ingredients and simmer for another 2–3 minutes.

3. Serve immediately with a light salad.

SHOPPING LIST

FENNEL BULB	$1.90
ONION	$0.13
GARLIC	$0.07
TILAPIA	$5.28
LEMON	$0.33
TOTAL	**$7.71**

POACHED ORANGE SCALLOPS WITH MINT

These poached scallops paired with the flavours of orange and mint make a wonderful main meal. If you prefer shrimp, go ahead. The dish tastes just as good. Either way, it's a restaurant-quality dish for less than $4.00 a person. Use fresh herbs for a bright flavour. SERVES 2

INGREDIENTS

- 1 orange, peeled and chopped
- 1 small onion, chopped
- 1 cup (250 mL) orange juice
- ½ cup (125 mL) light cream or whipping cream
- 1 Tbsp (15 mL) orange zest
- 1 tsp (5 mL) dried mint or 2 Tbsp (30 mL) chopped fresh mint
- ½ tsp (2 mL) dried basil or 1 Tbsp (15 mL) chopped fresh basil
- ½ tsp (2 mL) sea salt
- ½ tsp (2 mL) ground black pepper
- 1 lb (500 g) scallops

METHOD

1. Combine all of the ingredients, except the scallops, in a medium-sized saucepan and bring to a boil. Reduce the heat, add the scallops, and simmer for 5 minutes, or until the scallops are white and tender. Remove the scallops and set aside.
2. Cook the remaining mixture until the liquid reduces by half.
3. Return the scallops to the pan. Heat the scallops in the sauce for 1–2 minutes. Serve immediately.

SHOPPING LIST

ORANGE	$1.03
ONION	$0.13
SCALLOPS	$6.24
TOTAL	**$7.40**

SPICY GRILLED SHARK WITH SWEET ORANGE

Shark is a very meaty fish. I call it the steak of seafood. It's actually very economical and easy to find fresh or frozen in your local supermarket. If you can't find it, you can always use tuna or sea bass. SERVES 2

INGREDIENTS

2 cloves garlic, chopped

½ cup (125 mL) orange juice

3 Tbsp (45 mL) liquid honey

2 Tbsp (30 mL) olive oil

2 Tbsp (30 mL) lemon juice

½ tsp (2 mL) cayenne pepper

½ tsp (2 mL) dried basil

½ tsp (2 mL) dried thyme

½ tsp (2 mL) garlic powder

½ tsp (2 mL) onion powder

½ tsp (2 mL) sea salt

2 shark steaks, about 5–6 oz (150–175 g) each

1 seedless orange, sliced

METHOD

1. Combine all of the ingredients, except the shark and orange slices, in a large bowl. Set half the orange juice mixture aside. Place the shark steaks in a dish with the remaining portion. Marinate the shark for at least 15 minutes.

2. Grill both the shark and orange slices on high heat for 3–4 minutes per side, brushing the shark with the reserved orange juice mixture.

3. Serve immediately, spooning some of the remaining basting liquid on top of the shark.

SHOPPING LIST

GARLIC	$0.07
LEMON	$0.33
SHARK STEAKS	$6.82
ORANGE	$1.03
TOTAL	$8.25

PAN-SEARED CATFISH WITH TOMATOES & GREEN PEPPER

Catfish can be prepared in several ways. Here I am combining a bit of pan-searing in a tomato sauce and finishing with poaching. If you can't find catfish, use sole, orange roughy, or tilapia. SERVES 2

INGREDIENTS

2 Tbsp (30 mL) butter
1 green bell pepper, chopped
1 small onion, chopped
½ tsp (2 mL) sea salt
½ tsp (2 mL) ground black pepper
2 catfish fillets
one 28 oz (796 mL) can diced tomatoes
¼ cup (60 mL) vegetable stock
1 Tbsp (15 mL) Dijon mustard
1 tsp (5 mL) sugar
½ tsp (2 mL) dried basil
½ tsp (2 mL) dried thyme
½ tsp (2 mL) sea salt
½ tsp (2 mL) ground black pepper

METHOD

1. Melt 1 Tbsp (15 mL) of the butter in a medium-sized saucepan. Sauté the green pepper and onion for 2–3 minutes, or until translucent.
2. Salt and pepper the catfish. Using the same pan, add the remaining 1 Tbsp (15 mL) butter and sauté the fish for 2 minutes on each side.
3. Add all of the remaining ingredients. Bring to a boil then reduce the heat and simmer for another 3–5 minutes, basting with the sauce while cooking.

SHOPPING LIST

GREEN BELL PEPPER	$0.76
ONION	$0.13
CATFISH	$6.10
TOMATOES	$1.24
TOTAL	**$8.23**

BLACK BEAN TILAPIA WITH TOMATOES & FRESH BASIL

Fish is good for you, and when you combine it with the beans, it gives you lots of slow-burning energy. For a low-fat option, leave out the oil and just simmer in the sauce. SERVES 2

INGREDIENTS

- 2 Tbsp (30 mL) olive oil
- 1 small onion, chopped
- one 28 oz (796 mL) can diced tomatoes
- 1 cup (250 mL) cooked or canned black beans
- ½ cup (125 mL) fresh basil, chopped
- 2 Tbsp (30 mL) liquid honey
- 2 large tilapia fillets

METHOD

1. Heat the oil in a large saucepan. Sauté the onion for 2–3 minutes, or until translucent. Add all of the remaining ingredients, except the tilapia, mix well, and cook on medium heat for 5–8 minutes.
2. Place the tilapia fillets into the sauce and cover gently with the sauce, being careful not to break up the fish.
3. Simmer for 4–5 minutes, or until the flesh of the tilapia has turned white.

SHOPPING LIST

ONION	$0.13
CANNED TOMATOES	$1.24
BLACK BEANS	$0.80
FRESH BASIL	$0.99
TILAPIA	$5.28
TOTAL	$8.44

RED SNAPPER & WHITE BEANS WITH FRESH BASIL

I love the combination of white beans and red snapper. Healthy and hearty, it's what you want in a great dinner. You can replace the red snapper with cod, tilapia, or orange roughy. SERVES 2

INGREDIENTS

- 2 Tbsp (30 mL) olive oil
- 1 small onion, chopped
- 2 cloves garlic, chopped
- 1 cup (250 mL) cooked or canned white kidney beans
- 1 green bell pepper, chopped
- 1 cup (250 mL) vegetable stock
- ¼ cup (60 mL) chopped fresh basil
- 1 Tbsp (15 mL) chili powder
- ½ tsp (2 mL) sea salt
- ½ tsp (2 mL) ground black pepper
- 2 red snapper fillets

METHOD

1. Heat the olive oil in a medium-sized sauté pan. Add the onion, garlic, white kidney beans, and green bell pepper and sauté for 4–5 minutes.
2. Add the vegetable stock and fresh basil. Bring to a boil and reduce to a simmer.
3. Sprinkle the chili powder, salt, and pepper on the red snapper and add to the sauté pan. Cook, placing the bean mixture on top of the fish as it cooks through.

SHOPPING LIST

ONION	$0.13
GARLIC	$0.07
WHITE KIDNEY BEANS	$0.78
GREEN BELL PEPPER	$0.76
FRESH BASIL	$0.99
RED SNAPPER	$6.16
TOTAL	**$8.89**

GRILLED TIGER SHRIMP WITH LEMON & HONEY

Here's another dish you can make with either shrimp or scallops. You can find large-sized, usually frozen, tiger shrimp in your local supermarket. SERVES 2

INGREDIENTS

1 small red bell pepper, finely chopped

2 cloves garlic, chopped

½ cup (125 mL) lemon juice

2 Tbsp (30 mL) balsamic vinegar

2 Tbsp (30 mL) liquid honey

½ tsp (2 mL) dried thyme

½ tsp (2 mL) sea salt

½ tsp (2 mL) ground black pepper

8 large tiger shrimp, butterflied

lemon slices

¼ cup (60 mL) chopped fresh parsley

METHOD

1. Combine all of the ingredients, except the shrimp, lemon slices, and parsley, in a bowl. Coat both sides of the shrimp with the lemon juice mixture using a cooking brush.

2. Grill the shrimp on high heat for 2–3 minutes per side, basting with the remaining lemon juice mixture.

3. Serve immediately, garnished with the lemon slices and parsley.

SHOPPING LIST

RED BELL PEPPER	$0.96
GARLIC	$0.07
2 LEMONS	$0.66
TIGER SHRIMP	$6.49
FRESH PARSLEY	$0.99
TOTAL	**$9.17**

GRILLED SALMON SKEWERS WITH MIXED HERBS

The great thing about this recipe is that you can use other types of fish like tuna, swordfish, or shark. SERVES 2

INGREDIENTS

¼ cup (60 mL) olive oil

2 Tbsp (30 mL) lemon juice

2 Tbsp (30 mL) balsamic vinegar

½ tsp (2 mL) dried basil

½ tsp (2 mL) dried thyme

½ tsp (2 mL) dried oregano

½ tsp (2 mL) sea salt

½ tsp (2 mL) ground black pepper

8 cherry tomatoes

2 salmon steaks cut into 1-inch (2.5 cm) pieces

1 red bell pepper, cut into 4–6 pieces

1 green bell pepper, cut into 4–6 pieces

1 small onion, quartered

2 wooden skewers, soaked in warm water for 5 minutes

METHOD

1. Combine the olive oil, lemon juice, balsamic vinegar, dried herbs, salt, and pepper in a mixing bowl. Whisk well. Add all of the remaining ingredients and marinate for about 30 minutes.

2. Using the wooden skewers, alternate the ingredients like so: cherry tomato, then a piece of salmon, red pepper, onion, and green pepper. Continue the process until you have used all of the ingredients, ending with a cherry tomato.

3. On an outdoor or indoor grill on high, grill the skewers for about 6–8 minutes turning once.

SHOPPING LIST

LEMON	$0.22
CHERRY TOMATOES	$1.49
SALMON STEAKS	$5.80
RED BELL PEPPER	$1.56
GREEN BELL PEPPER	$0.76
ONION	$0.13
TOTAL	$9.96

POULTRY

DUCK WITH BALSAMIC ORANGE REDUCTION

Duck is a rich but delicate ingredient that gives you a restaurant-quality main dish every time.
Check for duck portions in the fresh or frozen sections of your supermarket.
Expensive, you say? Check out the cost! SERVES 2

INGREDIENTS

1 Tbsp (15 mL) olive oil
1 duck breast
½ tsp (2 mL) sea salt
½ tsp (2 mL) ground black
   pepper
1 orange, sliced
1 Tbsp (15 mL) olive oil
   (for reduction)
2 shallots, chopped
½ cup (125 mL) orange
   juice
1 Tbsp (15 mL) balsamic
   vinegar
1 tsp (5 mL) orange zest

METHOD

1. Heat the oil in a medium-sized ovenproof sauté pan. Salt and pepper the duck breast and brown each side for 4–5 minutes. Place the orange slices in the pan and put the pan in a pre-heated oven at 350°F (180°C) for 8–10 minutes.

2. Remove the duck and orange from the pan and let sit, covered, on a plate. Cut in half.

3. In the meantime, heat the olive oil in the same pan. Sauté the shallots. Add all of the remaining ingredients and reduce by half, or until it has reached a syrupy consistency. Plate the duck and drizzle with the balsamic-orange reduction.

SHOPPING LIST

DUCK BREAST	$4.39
ORANGE	$1.03
SHALLOTS	$1.99
TOTAL	$7.41

TURKEY SAUSAGE WITH FENNEL

This healthy alternative to a traditional barbecue satisfies summer cravings and costs only $3.73 per person. Turkey is a good economical option, but you can use any sausage of your choice to go with the great taste of fennel. SERVES 2

INGREDIENTS

1 fennel bulb, stalks and outside layer removed, cored, and sliced

1 red bell pepper, cut into large pieces

2 Tbsp (30 mL) olive oil

½ tsp (2 mL) sea salt

½ tsp (2 mL) ground black pepper

4 turkey sausages

2 Tbsp (30 mL) balsamic vinegar

1 tsp (5 mL) dried tarragon (optional)

METHOD

1. Brush the fennel slices and red bell pepper pieces with olive oil and sprinkle with salt and pepper.
2. Grill the turkey sausages, fennel, and red pepper on a pre-heated indoor or outdoor grill for 4–5 minutes, or until you have some grill marks. Turn once and grill for another 5–6 minutes, or until cooked through.
3. Place on a serving platter and drizzle the vegetables with balsamic vinegar. Sprinkle the entire dish with tarragon, if using.

SHOPPING LIST

FENNEL BULB	$1.90
RED BELL PEPPER	$1.56
TURKEY SAUSAGES	$3.99
TOTAL	**$7.45**

CRANBERRY CHICKEN WITH BALSAMIC REDUCTION

----

*The flavour combination of shallots and cranberries gives this recipe
a restaurant quality. Keep dried cranberries and cranberry juice on hand and you can have
this economical dish at home any day of the week.* SERVES 2

INGREDIENTS

2 Tbsp (30 mL) olive oil

2 chicken breasts, skin on,
bone-in

6 shallots, chopped

½ cup (125 mL) cranberry
juice

½ tsp (2 mL) dried basil

½ tsp (2 mL) sea salt

½ tsp (2 mL) ground black
pepper

¼ cup (60 mL) balsamic
vinegar

½ cup (125 mL) dried
cranberries

METHOD

1. Heat the oil in a medium-sized sauté pan. Brown the skin side
   of the chicken breast on medium heat for 8–10 minutes. Turn
   and brown the other side for another 8–10 minutes.

2. Add the shallots, cranberry juice, basil, salt, and pepper. Cook
   for another 4–5 minutes.

3. Add the balsamic vinegar and dried cranberries. Allow the
   sauce to reduce by half. Serve and drizzle with the reduction.

SHOPPING LIST

CHICKEN BREASTS	$4.37
SHALLOTS	$1.99
DRIED CRANBERRIES	$1.79
TOTAL	$8.15

MEDITERRANEAN STUFFED CHICKEN

When you crave a dish with rich Mediterranean flavours, you don't have to go out to a restaurant. You can make it easily at home and at a price you can afford. SERVES 2

INGREDIENTS

2 chicken breasts, skinned and boned

2 Tbsp (30 mL) Dijon mustard

4 cups (1 L) spinach

¼ cup (60 mL) olive oil

¼ cup (60 mL) balsamic vinegar

¼ cup (60 mL) cubed feta cheese

1 tsp (5 mL) chili powder

½ tsp (2 mL) garlic powder

½ tsp (2 mL) onion powder

½ tsp (2 mL) sea salt

½ tsp (2 mL) ground black pepper

METHOD

1. Butterfly the chicken. Coat the inside of the chicken breasts with mustard.

2. Chop the spinach and place it in a mixing bowl. Combine half the olive oil with the vinegar, feta cheese, chili powder, garlic powder, onion powder, sea salt, and pepper. Mix well. Place the spinach mixture on top of one breast and then place the other chicken breast on top. Coat liberally with the remaining olive oil.

3. Bake in a preheated oven at 350°F (180°C) for 40 minutes, basting once. Let sit for 5 minutes. Cut in half to serve.

SHOPPING LIST

CHICKEN	$4.37
SPINACH	$1.98
FETA CHEESE	$1.89
TOTAL	**$8.24**

SPINACH & RICOTTA STUFFED CHICKEN THIGHS

Spinach and ricotta cheese make a great stuffing for chicken. This recipe, when doubled or tripled, makes a nice dinner party dish to make at home or to take to a party. It's easy to prepare, and it won't break your budget. SERVES 2

INGREDIENTS

12 wooden toothpicks

2 cups (500 mL) baby spinach, chopped

½ cup (125 mL) ricotta cheese

1 tsp (5 mL) dried rosemary

6 chicken thighs, boned, skin on

2 Tbsp (30 mL) olive oil

½ tsp (2 mL) dried basil

½ tsp (2 mL) dried thyme

½ tsp (2 mL) sea salt

½ tsp (2 mL) ground black pepper

METHOD

1. Soak the toothpicks in warm water for 5 minutes.
2. Combine the spinach, ricotta, and rosemary in a large bowl. Mix well. Place the chicken thighs skin side down and evenly stuff the insides. (Alternatively, stuff with whole spinach leaves along with a dry ricotta and herb mixture that has been cubed.) Secure with toothpicks and place on a baking sheet.
3. Brush the olive oil on the skin of each of the chicken pieces. Sprinkle with basil, thyme, salt, and pepper and bake in a pre-heated oven at 350°F (180°C) for 25–30 minutes.

SHOPPING LIST

BABY SPINACH	$1.98
RICOTTA CHEESE	$1.84
CHICKEN THIGHS	$4.54
TOTAL	$8.36

SESAME CHICKEN WITH FRESH LIME

Sesame oil has a strong but wonderful flavour, especially when used in marinades, sauces, and salad dressings. The combination of the sesame oil and lime works well with chicken. And look at the cost. You can serve this restaurant-quality dish at home for just over $4.00 a person. You can also use turkey or four large portobello mushrooms instead of chicken. SERVES 2

INGREDIENTS

¼ cup (60 mL) sesame oil

2 Tbsp (30 mL) liquid honey

2 Tbsp (30 mL) soy sauce

juice of 4 limes

2 chicken breasts skin on, bone-in

2 limes, sliced

½ cup (125 mL) chopped fresh coriander (optional)

1 Tbsp (15 mL) sesame seeds or finely chopped walnuts, toasted

METHOD

1. Combine the sesame oil, honey, soy sauce, and lime juice in a bowl. Divide in half and set aside.

2. Place the lime slices in the bottom of an ovenproof pan. Gently brush the top of each chicken breast with half the liquid mixture and place the chicken overtop the lime slices.

3. Bake in a preheated oven at 350°F (180°C) for about 10 minutes. Baste the chicken using the reserved liquid and bake for another 20 minutes. Sprinkle with the chopped coriander and toasted sesame seeds (or walnuts) and bake for 5 minutes more.

```
        SHOPPING LIST
        ------------------------

LIMES                    $1.77
CHICKEN BREASTS          $4.37
FRESH CORIANDER          $0.94
SESAME SEEDS             $1.29
        _____

TOTAL                    $8.37
```

POACHED ORANGE TURKEY WITH MINT

Poached turkey is easy to make and offers a low-fat option. You can substitute fish or chicken in this recipe, and for a slightly more indulgent dish, add ¼ cup (60 mL) whipping cream to make a cream sauce. SERVES 2

INGREDIENTS

2 Tbsp (30 mL) olive oil

1 small turkey breast, skinned, boned, and cut in half

4 shallots, chopped

1 small red bell pepper, chopped

2 cups (500 mL) orange juice

¼ cup (60 mL) balsamic vinegar

1 Tbsp (15 mL) orange zest

1 tsp (5 mL) dried mint

½ tsp (2 mL) ground black pepper

½ tsp (2 mL) sea salt

METHOD

1. Heat the oil in a medium-sized sauté pan. Gently brown the turkey on both sides for 8–10 minutes. Add the shallots and sauté for another 2 minutes.

2. Add all of the remaining ingredients. Bring to a boil then reduce the heat. Simmer for about 10 minutes, turning once.

3. Serve, using the orange poaching mixture as a sauce.

SHOPPING LIST

TURKEY BREAST	$5.49
SHALLOTS	$1.99
RED BELL PEPPER	$0.96
ORANGE	$1.03
TOTAL	**$9.47**

BAKED TOMATO CHICKEN WITH BASIL & PARMESAN

Simple ingredients give this baked chicken dish a kick of flavour for only $4.50 a person. You can also use pork instead of chicken. SERVES 2

INGREDIENTS

- 2 Tbsp (30 mL) olive oil
- 2 chicken breasts, skinned and boned
- ½ tsp (2 mL) dried rosemary
- ½ tsp (2 mL) sea salt
- ½ tsp (2 mL) ground black pepper
- 1 large tomato, sliced
- 1 small bunch fresh basil, chopped
- 2 Tbsp (30 mL) grated Parmesan cheese

METHOD

1. Heat the oil in a medium-sized ovenproof sauté pan. Sprinkle the chicken breasts with the rosemary, salt, and pepper and brown for 8–10 minutes, turning once.
2. Remove the sauté pan from the stove and evenly distribute the tomato slices, fresh basil, and Parmesan on top of the chicken.
3. Bake in a preheated oven at 350°F (180°C) for 10–15 minutes, or until brown.

SHOPPING LIST

CHICKEN BREASTS	$4.37
TOMATO	$0.88
FRESH BASIL	$0.99
PARMESAN CHEESE	$2.59
TOTAL	$8.83

EASY COQ AU VIN

A slowly simmered coq au vin–type dish allows all of the wonderful flavours to dance together. SERVES 2

INGREDIENTS

3 Tbsp (45 mL) olive oil

4 chicken thighs

4 chicken drumsticks

1 cup (250 mL) red cooking wine

1 red onion, chopped

1 green bell pepper, chopped

1 carrot, peeled and chopped

2 cloves garlic, chopped

one 14 oz (398 mL) can diced tomatoes

1 cup (250 mL) chicken stock

2 Tbsp (30 mL) sugar

½ tsp (2 mL) dried basil

½ tsp (2 mL) dried rosemary

½ tsp (2 mL) dried thyme

½ tsp (2 mL) sea salt

½ tsp (2 mL) ground black pepper

METHOD

1. Heat the oil in a large saucepan. Brown the chicken pieces for 4–5 minutes. Add the wine and deglaze the pan.
2. Add all of the remaining ingredients. Bring to a boil then reduce the heat.
3. Simmer for 15–20 minutes until the chicken and vegetables are cooked.

SHOPPING LIST

CHICKEN THIGHS	$3.84
CHICKEN DRUMSTICKS	$3.65
RED ONION	$0.40
GREEN BELL PEPPER	$0.76
CARROT	$0.19
GARLIC	$0.07
CANNED TOMATOES	$0.87
TOTAL	$9.78

STIR-FRIED CHICKEN WITH ASPARAGUS, GINGER & TOMATO

Chicken thighs are not only economical, they also work great in a stir-fry. Deboned and skinned, they offer a low-fat meal that has plenty of flavour. If you're a meat lover, just substitute sliced pork for the chicken. SERVES 2

INGREDIENTS

2 Tbsp (30 mL) olive oil

6 chicken thighs, skinned, boned, and sliced

1 red onion, chopped

1 bunch asparagus, rinsed well and cut into pieces

1 large tomato, chopped

2 Tbsp (30 mL) soy sauce

1 tsp (5 mL) fresh ginger, chopped

½ tsp (2 mL) dried basil

½ tsp (2 mL) whole cumin seeds

½ cup (125 mL) chopped fresh parsley

METHOD

1. Heat the oil in a medium-sized sauté pan or wok. Gently sauté the chicken for 4–5 minutes.

2. Add the onion and asparagus and continue to sauté for another 4–5 minutes.

3. Add all of the remaining ingredients, except the parsley, and continue to stir-fry for 2–3 minutes. Sprinkle with the parsley and serve.

SHOPPING LIST

CHICKEN THIGHS	$4.54
RED ONION	$0.40
ASPARAGUS	$2.76
TOMATO	$0.88
FRESH GINGER	$0.25
FRESH PARSLEY	$0.99
TOTAL	$9.82

MEAT

GRILLED STEAK WITH MUSHROOM & APPLE "CAVIAR"

Grilling indoors has become very popular and easy. If you keep your pantry stocked with essential items (see page xi), this steak costs less than $3.00 a person, but if you want to go a bit more high-end, buy sirloin or T-bone steak, or even tenderloin. SERVES 2

INGREDIENTS

1 tsp (5 mL) ground black pepper

½ tsp (2 mL) dried basil

½ tsp (2 mL) dried oregano

½ tsp (2 mL) dried rosemary

½ tsp (2 mL) dried thyme

½ tsp (2 mL) sea salt

2 Tbsp (30 mL) olive oil

2 strip loin steaks

1 cup (250 mL) Mushroom & Apple "Caviar" (page 148)

METHOD

1. In a small bowl, mix together all of the dried ingredients. Brush the oil over both sides of the steaks. Sprinkle the dried ingredient mixture over the steaks. Let them stand for at least 30 minutes.

2. Grill the steaks on high heat for 6–8 minutes per side if you prefer your steak rare, or 12–15 minutes per side for well done. (The grilling time also depends on the thickness of the steak.)

3. Warm the mushroom and apple "caviar" in a saucepan. Spoon over the steaks and serve.

SHOPPING LIST

STRIP LOIN STEAKS	$5.64
TOTAL	$5.64

PORK TENDERLOIN MEDALLIONS WITH APPLE & CINNAMON

Pork tenderloin with apples is a great combination. The recipe is easy to prepare and gives you that restaurant quality for only $6.00. If you like, you can substitute chicken for the pork. SERVES 2

INGREDIENTS

2 Tbsp (30 mL) olive oil

1 lb (500 g) pork tenderloin cut into 1-inch-thick (2.5 cm) medallions

1 small onion, chopped

1 apple, cored and sliced

½ cup (125 mL) applesauce

½ cup (125 mL) apple juice

2 Tbsp (30 mL) balsamic vinegar

½ tsp (2 mL) cinnamon

½ tsp (2 mL) dried basil

½ tsp (2 mL) sea salt

½ tsp (2 mL) ground black pepper

METHOD

1. Heat the oil in a large sauté pan. Sauté the pork for 3–4 minutes.

2. Add the onion and apple. Sauté the mixture for 4–5 minutes.

3. Add all of the remaining ingredients. Bring to a boil then reduce the heat. Simmer for 10–15 minutes, or until the liquid is reduced by half. Serve.

SHOPPING LIST

PORK TENDERLOIN	$5.28
ONION	$0.13
APPLE	$0.59
TOTAL	$6.00

STEAK WITH SWEET ONION RELISH

Steaks are always tastier when combined with a relish or a sauce of some kind. SERVES 2

INGREDIENTS

1 lb (500 g) inside round steak, cut in half, or 2 strip loin steaks

½ cup (125 mL) soy sauce

¼ cup (60 mL) olive oil (for the marinade)

1 Tbsp (15 mL) sugar

2 shallots, chopped

3 cloves garlic, chopped

2 Tbsp (30 mL) olive oil (for the onions)

2 onions, sliced

½ cup (125 mL) chicken or beef stock

2 Tbsp (30 mL) sugar

1 Tbsp (15 mL) Dijon mustard

½ tsp (2 mL) dried basil

½ tsp (2 mL) dried thyme

½ tsp (2 mL) sea salt

½ tsp (2 mL) ground black pepper

METHOD

1. Place the 2 pieces of steak inside a large freezer bag. Add the soy sauce, olive oil, sugar, shallots, and garlic. Close the bag and mix well, turning the meat to coat. Marinate in the refrigerator for 24 hours.

2. Grill the steaks on high heat for 4–5 minutes per side for medium doneness, or 8–10 minutes per side if you prefer your steaks well done. Remove the meat from the heat and let sit.

3. Heat the oil in a saucepan. Sauté the onions for 8–10 minutes, or until translucent. Add all of the remaining ingredients. Bring to a boil then reduce the heat. Simmer for about 10 minutes. Serve on top of the grilled steak.

SHOPPING LIST

ROUND STEAK	$4.69
SHALLOTS	$1.99
GARLIC	$0.07
ONIONS	$0.26
TOTAL	$7.01

PEPPERED STRIP LOIN WITH CRANBERRY REDUCTION

Steak is my favourite food. When I was growing up, we always had steak on Saturdays, and it's a memory I am so fond of. This recipe is a tribute to "steak Saturday." You can replace the strip loin with other cuts of beef, such as T-bone or sirloin. If using other cuts, marinate overnight. SERVES 2

INGREDIENTS

- 2 strip loin steaks, 5 oz (150 g) each
- 2 Tbsp (30 mL) olive oil
- ½ tsp (2 mL) sea salt
- 2 Tbsp (30 mL) freshly ground black pepper (to coat the steaks)
- 1 cup (250 mL) cranberry juice
- 2 Tbsp (30 mL) cranberry jam
- ½ cup (125 mL) dried cranberries
- 2 Tbsp (30 mL) balsamic vinegar
- ½ tsp (2 mL) ground black pepper (for the sauce)

METHOD

1. Brush the steaks with the oil. Coat them with the salt and pepper. Let stand for at least 30 minutes.
2. Grill the steaks on high heat for 5–6 minutes per side for medium doneness, or for 10–12 minutes per side if you prefer your steak well done.
3. Combine the cranberry juice, jam, dried cranberries, balsamic vinegar, and pepper in a large saucepan. Bring to a boil then reduce the heat. Simmer for 10–15 minutes, or until reduced by half. Serve on top of the steaks.

SHOPPING LIST

STRIP LOIN STEAKS	$5.64
CRANBERRY JAM	$1.67
DRIED CRANBERRIES	$1.79
TOTAL	$9.10

ORANGE BEEF SAUTÉED WITH BELL PEPPERS & GINGER

This Asian-inspired dish is healthy and delicious and tastes just as good with turkey strips instead of sliced beef. And all for just over $4.50 a person! SERVES 2

INGREDIENTS

2 Tbsp (30 mL) olive oil

2 cloves garlic, chopped

1½ lb (750 g) thinly sliced flank or round steak

1 red bell pepper, sliced

1 green bell pepper, sliced

2 tsp (10 mL) fresh ginger, minced

½ orange, sliced

2 tsp (10 mL) orange zest

½ cup (125 mL) soy sauce

2 Tbsp (30 mL) liquid honey

2 tsp (10 mL) sesame oil

METHOD

1. Heat the oil in a large sauté pan. Gently sauté the garlic without burning. Add the sliced beef and continue to sauté for 4–5 minutes.
2. Add the bell peppers, ginger, and orange and zest. Continue to cook for 2–3 minutes.
3. Add the soy sauce, honey, and sesame oil and cook for 2 more minutes.

SHOPPING LIST

GARLIC	$0.07
BEEF	$5.61
RED BELL PEPPER	$1.56
GREEN BELL PEPPER	$0.76
FRESH GINGER	$0.25
ORANGE	$1.03
TOTAL	$9.28

SAUTÉED LAMB WITH APRICOTS & HERBS

I like to combine savoury and sweet tastes. Nothing embodies that better than lamb and dried apricots. Mind you, apricots work just as nicely with stewing beef. SERVES 2

INGREDIENTS

2 Tbsp (30 mL) olive oil

1 lb (500 g) stewing lamb, cut into pieces, or 4 bone-in lamb pieces

1 cup (250 mL) beef stock

1 small onion, chopped

½ cup (125 mL) dried apricots, chopped

½ cup (125 mL) apple juice

2 Tbsp (30 mL) apricot jam

2 Tbsp (30 mL) balsamic vinegar

½ tsp (2 mL) dried basil

½ tsp (2 mL) dried oregano

½ tsp (2 mL) dried thyme

½ tsp (2 mL) sea salt

½ tsp (2 mL) ground black pepper

METHOD

1. Heat the oil in a large sauté pan. Brown the lamb for 5–8 minutes, stirring frequently.

2. Add all of the remaining ingredients. Bring the mixture to a boil then reduce the heat.

3. Simmer for 10–15 minutes, or until the liquid begins to thicken. Serve immediately.

```
         SHOPPING LIST
         ----------------------

STEWING LAMB            $5.40
ONION                   $0.11
DRIED APRICOTS          $2.99
APRICOT JAM             $1.49
         ======================
TOTAL                   $9.99
```

WASABI BURGERS WITH GREEN PEPPER & PARMESAN

These wasabi burgers will wow your family and friends. I like to shape my burgers in squares to be different. Ground chicken or turkey works just as well. SERVES 2

INGREDIENTS

1 lb (500 g) lean ground beef

1 small green bell pepper, finely chopped

1 small onion, finely chopped

1 egg

¼ cup (60 mL) panko breadcrumbs

¼ cup (60 mL) grated Parmesan cheese

2 Tbsp (30 mL) wasabi paste

2 Tbsp (30 mL) hoisin sauce

½ tsp (2 mL) dried basil

½ tsp (2 mL) dried thyme

½ tsp (2 mL) ground black pepper

½ tsp (2 mL) sea salt

METHOD

1. Place all of the ingredients in a large bowl. Mix well. Shape into 4 large patties.
2. Grill the burgers on high for about 5 minutes each side.
3. Serve immediately with a variety of condiments.

SHOPPING LIST

LEAN GROUND BEEF	$3.59
GREEN BELL PEPPER	$0.51
ONION	$0.13
PARMESAN CHEESE	$0.65
TOTAL	$4.88

KENNY'S BEEF STEW TO BRAG ABOUT

Beef stew is the ultimate comfort food, and when you make it in late summer or early autumn using freshly harvested vegetables, it's even more economical than the cost below. If you don't eat red meat, just use turkey breasts, cut into pieces. SERVES 2

INGREDIENTS

- 2 Tbsp (30 mL) olive oil
- 1 lb (500 g) stewing beef, cut into pieces
- 2 potatoes, peeled and cubed
- 1 turnip, peeled and cubed
- 1 small onion, chopped
- 2 carrots, peeled and cubed
- 2 celery stalks, chopped
- 3 cups (750 mL) beef stock
- 2 Tbsp (30 mL) liquid honey
- 1 Tbsp (15 mL) Dijon mustard
- 1 tsp (5 mL) Worcestershire sauce
- ½ tsp (2 mL) dried basil
- ½ tsp (2 mL) dried rosemary
- ½ tsp (2 mL) sea salt
- ½ tsp (2 mL) ground black pepper

METHOD

1. Heat the oil in a large saucepan. Brown the beef, constantly turning, for 8–10 minutes.
2. Add all of the remaining ingredients and bring to a boil.
3. Reduce to a simmer for 15–20 minutes.

SHOPPING LIST

STEWING BEEF	$5.44
POTATOES	$0.72
TURNIP	$0.45
ONION	$0.13
CARROTS	$0.38
CELERY	$1.67
TOTAL	**$8.79**

LAMB CHOPS WITH PEARS

Lamb is one of my favourite meats to prepare for dinner. Make sure that you never overcook lamb because it can dry out—I find it's best a little on the rare side. You can replace the pears with apples or with oranges cut into wedges (and replace the pear nectar as well). SERVES 2

INGREDIENTS

2 Tbsp (30 mL) olive oil

4 lamb chops

½ tsp (2 mL) dried rosemary

½ tsp (2 mL) dried thyme

pinch of sea salt

pinch of black pepper

2 pears, cored and sliced

2 whole cloves garlic

½ cup (125 mL) pear nectar

1 Tbsp (15 mL) sugar

METHOD

1. Heat 1 Tbsp (15 mL) of the olive oil in a large sauté pan. Brown the lamb chops for 5 minutes per side, or until they are cooked through. Season the chops with the rosemary, thyme, salt, and pepper. Remove the lamb chops from the pan and keep them warm.

2. Heat the remaining 1 Tbsp (15 mL) olive oil in the pan. Stir in all of the remaining ingredients. Cook on medium heat until the pears are softened and lightly browned.

3. Pour the warm pear mixture over the lamb chops. Serve immediately.

SHOPPING LIST

LAMB CHOPS	$7.57
PEARS	$1.38
GARLIC	$0.07
TOTAL	$9.02

STIR-FRIED PORK WITH GINGER, RED PEPPER & RAISINS

Stir-fries are always great! This combination is savoury, sweet, and satisfying.
For a low-fat option, use chicken instead. SERVES 2

INGREDIENTS

2 Tbsp (30 mL) olive oil

4 pork loin chops, cut into thin strips

3 cloves garlic, sliced

1 Tbsp (15 mL) finely chopped ginger

½ cup (125 mL) raisins

1 red bell pepper, sliced

1 cup (250 mL) snow peas

1 bunch green onions, chopped

2 Tbsp (30 mL) soy sauce

2 tsp (10 mL) sesame oil

METHOD

1. Heat the oil in a large sauté pan or wok. Brown the pork for 2–4 minutes.

2. Add the garlic, ginger, raisins, red pepper, snow peas, and half the green onions. Continue to sauté for another 4 minutes.

3. Make a hole in the centre of the vegetables and pork and add the soy sauce and sesame oil. Mix and continue to cook for another 2 minutes. Add the remaining green onions.

SHOPPING LIST

PORK LOIN CHOPS	$4.37
GARLIC	$0.07
FRESH GINGER	$0.25
RAISINS	$0.80
RED BELL PEPPER	$1.56
SNOW PEAS	$1.49
GREEN ONIONS	$0.62
TOTAL	$9.16

SPICY ASIAN BEEF STIR-FRY WITH A HINT OF ORANGE

Stir-frying is quick and easy and requires a minimum amount of fat so it's also healthy. To make this stir-fry especially delicious, marinate the beef for one hour before cooking. This one squeaks in just under the $10 limit, but it's still way cheaper than eating out. You can replace the beef with chicken, turkey, pork, or jumbo shrimp and it's just as tasty. SERVES 2

INGREDIENTS

3 Tbsp (45 mL) olive oil

1 lb (500 g) inside round steak strips

2 cloves garlic, chopped

1 green bell pepper, sliced

1 small onion, sliced

½ cup (125 mL) broccoli florets

½ cup (125 mL) cauliflower florets

½ tsp (2 mL) orange zest

½ tsp (2 mL) dried basil

½ tsp (2 mL) dried thyme

½ tsp (2 mL) red pepper flakes

¼ cup (60 mL) orange juice

¼ cup (60 mL) soy sauce

2 Tbsp (30 mL) liquid honey

1 Tbsp (15 mL) dried chives

METHOD

1. Heat 1 Tbsp (15 mL) of the oil in a large sauté pan. Sauté the beef on high heat for 10 minutes. Remove the beef; set aside.
2. Wipe out the pan. Stir-fry the garlic, vegetables, zest, herbs, and hot red pepper flakes in the remaining 2 Tbsp (30 mL) oil on high heat for 5 minutes.
3. Add the orange juice, soy sauce, honey, and reserved beef. Simmer the mixture for 3–5 minutes. Add the chives and serve immediately.

SHOPPING LIST

ROUND STEAK	$4.89
GARLIC	$0.07
GREEN BELL PEPPER	$0.49
ONION	$0.13
BROCCOLI	$1.97
CAULIFLOWER	$2.29
TOTAL	$9.84

VEGETARIAN

MEDITERRANEAN BROCCOLI IN A ROSE SAUCE WITH FINE HERBS

This delicious broccoli dish is quick and easy to make and only costs $2.00 a serving. You can substitute cauliflower for the broccoli. SERVES 2

INGREDIENTS

3 Tbsp (45 mL) olive oil

2 cloves garlic, chopped

1 large head broccoli, cut into florets

1 large onion, chopped

1 carrot, peeled and chopped

one 28 oz (796 mL) can diced tomatoes

½ cup (125 mL) vegetable stock

2 Tbsp (30 mL) sugar

1 tsp (5 mL) chili powder

½ tsp (2 mL) dried rosemary

½ tsp (2 mL) dried basil

½ tsp (2 mL) sea salt

½ tsp (2 mL) ground black pepper

½ cup (125 mL) light cream or whipping cream

cherry tomatoes, halved (optional)

METHOD

1. Heat the oil in a large pot and sauté the garlic and all of the vegetables for 5–6 minutes.

2. Add all of the remaining ingredients, except the cream. Bring to a boil then reduce the heat. Simmer for about 5 minutes.

3. Add the cream, mix well to a creamy texture, and serve. Garnish with cherry tomatoes, if desired.

```
            SHOPPING LIST
            ----------------------
GARLIC                      $0.07
BROCCOLI                    $1.97
ONION                       $0.43
CARROT                      $0.19
CANNED TOMATOES             $1.24
            ======================
TOTAL                       $3.90
```

ORANGE BOK CHOY WITH HOISIN & TARRAGON

Bok choy is one of the most delicate vegetables you can use in a stir-fry. When you combine it with oranges, it brings a new taste to a traditional Asian dish found in many fine restaurants. This homemade dish at just over $4.00 for two people is every bit as good. SERVES 2

INGREDIENTS

3 Tbsp (45 mL) olive oil
1 small onion, sliced
2 cloves garlic, chopped
1 red bell pepper, sliced
1 orange, peeled and sliced
1½ lb (750 g) bok choy
   (about 6 small), halved
¼ cup (60 mL) hoisin sauce
½ cup (125 mL) orange
   juice
1 tsp (5 mL) orange zest
2 Tbsp (30 mL) soy sauce
2 Tbsp (30 mL) liquid
   honey
1 tsp (5 mL) dried tarragon
½ cup (125 mL) green
   onions, chopped

METHOD

1. Heat the oil in a wok or large sauté pan over high heat. Add the onion, garlic, bell pepper, and orange and sauté for 2–3 minutes. Add the bok choy and sauté for 4–5 minutes more.
2. Mix the hoisin, orange juice, orange zest, soy sauce, and liquid honey in a bowl. Make a hole in the centre of the bok choy mixture and pour in the wet mixture. Continue to sauté, mixing well, for 2–3 minutes. Add the tarragon and sauté for another 2 minutes.
3. Sprinkle the green onions on the bok choy and serve.

SHOPPING LIST

ONION	$0.13
GARLIC	$0.07
RED BELL PEPPER	$1.56
ORANGE	$1.03
BOK CHOY	$0.99
GREEN ONIONS	$0.62
TOTAL	$4.40

WARM POTATOES, PEAR & PECANS ON MIXED GREENS

This recipe makes a great meal, especially in the spring and summer when you can add some grilled fish. SERVES 2

INGREDIENTS

1½ lb (750 g) white- or red-skinned potatoes, unpeeled

2 Tbsp (30 mL) lemon juice

1 pear, cored and sliced

1 tsp (5 mL) Dijon mustard

2 Tbsp (30 mL) white wine vinegar

2 Tbsp (30 mL) sesame oil

½ tsp (2 mL) sea salt

½ tsp (2 mL) ground black pepper

2 cups (500 mL) mixed salad greens

2 Tbsp (30 mL) chopped pecans or walnuts

2 tsp (10 mL) toasted sesame seeds (optional)

METHOD

1. Boil the potatoes in lightly salted water for 10–15 minutes. Drain and set aside.

2. Drizzle the lemon juice on the pear to prevent browning. Whisk the mustard, wine vinegar, sesame oil, salt, and pepper until smooth.

3. Take half the dressing and mix with the warm potatoes. Place the potatoes on top of the greens and arrange the pear slices along the side. Sprinkle with pecans (or walnuts) and toasted sesame seeds (if using) and serve.

SHOPPING LIST

POTATOES	$2.48
LEMON	$0.33
PEAR	$0.69
SALAD GREENS	$1.79
PECANS	$1.50
TOTAL	$6.79

SWEET POTATO PANCAKES WITH MAPLE SYRUP & CINNAMON

These sweet potato pancakes make for a different, but delicious, dinner. You can also prepare any type of fish and serve it on top of the pancakes. SERVES 2

INGREDIENTS

- 2 sweet potatoes, peeled and cut into chunks
- 1 small egg white
- ¼ cup (60 mL) maple syrup
- 3 Tbsp (45 mL) self-raising flour
- 2 Tbsp (30 mL) milk
- ½ tsp (2 mL) cinnamon
- ½ tsp (2 mL) dried thyme
- 2 Tbsp (30 mL) vegetable oil
- ½ cup (125 mL) sour cream

METHOD

1. Place the sweet potatoes in a large saucepan and cover with lightly salted water. Bring to a boil then cover and reduce the heat. Simmer for 15 minutes, or until tender. Drain the potatoes and transfer to a large bowl.
2. Add all of the remaining ingredients, except the vegetable oil and sour cream.
3. Heat the oil in a large sauté pan and make the pancakes with large spoonfuls of batter. Flip once, cooking for 3–4 minutes on each side. Serve with a dollop of sour cream.

SHOPPING LIST

SWEET POTATOES	$1.38
MAPLE SYRUP	$2.99
FLOUR	$0.99
TOTAL	**$5.36**

CURRY VEGETABLE STEW WITH COCONUT MILK & FRESH CORIANDER

This curry vegetable stew is a collection of nutritious vegetables, and it costs just over $5.00. You can make it even more economical by using vegetables from your own garden. SERVES 2

INGREDIENTS

3 Tbsp (45 mL) olive oil

1 small onion, chopped

2 cloves garlic, chopped

1 green bell pepper, chopped

2 medium potatoes, peeled and cubed

1 carrot, chopped

1 medium zucchini, sliced

1 cup (250 mL) button mushrooms, sliced

4 cups (1 L) vegetable stock

2 Tbsp (30 mL) mild curry powder

2 Tbsp (30 mL) soy sauce

½ cup (125 mL) coconut milk

½ cup (125 mL) chopped fresh coriander

METHOD

1. Heat the oil in a medium-sized pot. Add all of the vegetables and gently sauté for 4–5 minutes.

2. Add all of the remaining ingredients, except the coconut milk and coriander. Bring to a boil then reduce the heat. Simmer for about 15 minutes.

3. Add the coconut milk and fresh coriander and serve.

SHOPPING LIST

ONION	$0.13
GARLIC	$0.07
GREEN BELL PEPPER	$0.76
POTATOES	$0.72
CARROT	$0.19
ZUCCHINI	$0.53
MUSHROOMS	$1.73
FRESH CORIANDER	$0.94
TOTAL	$5.07

SAUTÉED PORTOBELLO MUSHROOMS & ONION IN A BALSAMIC REDUCTION

Portobello mushrooms are a hearty vegetarian substitute for meat in several recipes. In this recipe, you can replace the portobellos with any other mushroom of your choice—such as button, shiitake, or cremini. SERVES 2

INGREDIENTS

- 2 Tbsp (30 mL) olive oil
- 3 large portobello mushrooms, cleaned, cut into lengths
- 2 medium red onions, sliced
- 1 red bell pepper, sliced
- ¼ cup (60 mL) balsamic vinegar
- ½ tsp (2 mL) dried basil
- ½ tsp (2 mL) dried rosemary
- ½ tsp (2 mL) chili powder
- ½ tsp (2 mL) sea salt
- ½ tsp (2 mL) ground black pepper

METHOD

1. Heat the oil in a large pot. Sauté all of the vegetables for 4–5 minutes.
2. Add all of the remaining ingredients and sauté for 3–4 more minutes to allow the balsamic vinegar to reduce.
3. Serve immediately.

SHOPPING LIST

PORTOBELLO MUSHROOMS	$4.29
RED ONIONS	$0.80
RED BELL PEPPER	$1.56
TOTAL	**$6.65**

BROILED PORTOBELLO MUSHROOM WITH PEAR & PROVOLONE

The mushroom and pear combination gives this dish a unique flavour that is both filling and satisfying. SERVES 2

INGREDIENTS

2 Tbsp (30 mL) olive oil

4 large portobello mushroom caps, cleaned

2 Tbsp (30 mL) Dijon mustard

1 Tbsp (15 mL) balsamic vinegar

1 pear, cored and sliced

4 slices Provolone cheese

1 tsp (5 mL) dried thyme

½ tsp (2 mL) ground black pepper

METHOD

1. Heat the oil in an ovenproof sauté pan and sauté the topside of the portobello mushrooms for 2–4 minutes, or until brown.

2. Evenly distribute first the Dijon mustard and then the balsamic vinegar into the cap of the mushrooms. Layer each mushroom with pear slices and cover with the Provolone cheese. Sprinkle with the thyme and pepper.

3. Broil for 3–5 minutes, or until the Provolone starts to bubble and brown. Serve.

SHOPPING LIST

PORTOBELLO MUSHROOMS	$4.29
PEAR	$0.69
PROVOLONE CHEESE	$1.84
TOTAL	$6.82

EGGPLANT & TOMATO STACKERS

Eggplant is one of those vegetables you're not sure what to do with sometimes. This solution is delicious and quite impressive when served. SERVES 2

INGREDIENTS

1 egg

¼ cup (60 mL) milk

½ cup (125 mL) panko breadcrumbs

½ tsp (2 mL) ground cumin

½ tsp (2 mL) sea salt

½ tsp (2 mL) ground black pepper

2 Tbsp (30 mL) olive oil

1 small eggplant, unpeeled, cut into ½-inch (1 cm) slices

1 large tomato, sliced

¼ cup (60 mL) fresh basil, chopped

1 ball mozzarella, sliced

METHOD

1. Combine the egg and milk and mix in a bowl. In a separate bowl combine the panko breadcrumbs, cumin, salt, and pepper and mix.

2. Heat the oil in a large, ovenproof sauté pan over medium heat. Dip the eggplant first into the wet mixture, then into the dry mixture. Cook until golden brown, turning once.

3. Once the eggplant is turned, put a slice of tomato, some basil, and a slice of mozzarella on top of each eggplant slice. Place the stackers into a preheated oven at 350°F (180°C) for 5–8 minutes or until the mozzarella cheese starts to melt. Serve immediately.

SHOPPING LIST

EGGPLANT	$1.49
TOMATO	$0.88
FRESH BASIL	$0.99
MOZZARELLA BALL	$2.39
TOTAL	$5.75

PASTA

SPAGHETTI WITH OLIVES, FETA & ROSEMARY

*My favourite pasta is spaghetti, and when I add olives and feta cheese
I have a truly European dinner.* SERVES 2

INGREDIENTS

1 lb (500 g) spaghetti

2 Tbsp (30 mL) olive oil

2 cloves garlic, chopped

1 small green bell pepper, chopped

1 small red onion, chopped

½ cup (125 mL) black olives, sliced

½ cup (125 mL) vegetable or chicken stock

½ cup (125 mL) white cooking wine

2 Tbsp (30 mL) lemon juice

½ tsp (2 mL) dried basil

½ tsp (2 mL) dried rosemary

½ tsp (2 mL) sea salt

½ tsp (2 mL) ground black pepper

½ cup (125 mL) cubed or crumbled feta cheese

METHOD

1. Bring a large pot of salted water to a boil. Cook the pasta for 8–10 minutes, or until *al dente*.

2. While the pasta is cooking, heat the oil in a large saucepan. Sauté the garlic, green bell pepper, and onion for about 2 minutes. Add all of the remaining ingredients, except the feta cheese. Sauté for 5–6 minutes.

3. Drain the pasta and return it to the pot. Pour the sauce over the pasta and toss to coat. Stir the feta cheese into the pasta. Serve immediately.

SHOPPING LIST

SPAGHETTI	$1.16
GARLIC	$0.07
GREEN BELL PEPPER	$0.51
RED ONION	$0.33
OLIVES	$1.69
LEMON	$0.33
FETA CHEESE	$1.89
TOTAL	$5.98

BOW-TIE PASTA WITH GOAT CHEESE, GARLIC & BASIL

This is an incredibly simple recipe. The combination of goat cheese and garlic works great with pasta. If you like, you can use feta cheese instead. SERVES 2

INGREDIENTS

1 lb (500 g) bow-tie pasta

3 Tbsp (45 mL) olive oil

4 cloves garlic, chopped

1 small red bell pepper, chopped

4 medium shallots, chopped

½ cup (125 mL) vegetable or chicken stock

½ cup (125 mL) white cooking wine

2 Tbsp (30 mL) lemon juice

½ tsp (2 mL) dried basil

½ tsp (2 mL) sea salt

½ tsp (2 mL) ground black pepper

½ cup (125 mL) crumbled goat cheese

METHOD

1. Bring a large pot of salted water to a boil. Cook the pasta for 8–10 minutes, or until *al dente*.

2. While the pasta is cooking, heat the oil in the pan. Sauté the garlic, red bell pepper, and shallots for about 2 minutes. Add all of the remaining ingredients, except the goat cheese. Sauté for 5–6 minutes.

3. Drain the pasta and return it to the pot. Pour the sauce over the pasta and toss to coat. Stir the goat cheese into the pasta. Serve immediately.

```
         SHOPPING LIST
         ------------------------

BOW-TIE PASTA            $0.99
GARLIC                   $0.07
RED BELL PEPPER          $0.96
SHALLOTS                 $1.99
LEMON                    $0.33
GOAT CHEESE              $2.60
         _____

TOTAL                    $6.94
```

PASTA WITH SAUSAGE, RED PEPPERS & HERBS

I use Italian sausage in this recipe, but you can try any of the several different types that are available. Try a sausage you've never had before or replace the sausage with cubed chicken. SERVES 2

INGREDIENTS

1 lb (500 g) penne

2 Tbsp (30 mL) olive oil

2 medium shallots, chopped

1 red bell pepper, chopped

2 Italian sausages, sliced

½ cup (125 mL) vegetable stock

one 14 oz (398 mL) can diced tomatoes

½ cup (125 mL) light cream or whipping cream

2 Tbsp (30 mL) balsamic vinegar

1 tsp (5 mL) dried dill

½ tsp (2 mL) dried basil

½ tsp (2 mL) dried thyme

½ tsp (2 mL) sea salt

½ tsp (2 mL) ground black pepper

METHOD

1. Bring a large pot of salted water to a boil. Cook the pasta for 8–10 minutes, or until *al dente*.

2. While the pasta is cooking, heat the oil in a small pot. Gently sauté the shallots and red bell pepper for 2 minutes. Add the sausage, stock, and tomatoes. Cook for 2 minutes. Add all of the remaining ingredients. Simmer the sauce for 5–6 minutes, or until it thickens.

3. Drain the pasta and return it to the pot. Pour the sauce over the pasta. Serve immediately.

SHOPPING LIST

PENNE	$1.22
SHALLOTS	$1.99
RED BELL PEPPER	$1.56
ITALIAN SAUSAGE	$1.60
CANNED TOMATOES	$0.87
TOTAL	$7.24

BOW-TIE PASTA WITH CHICKEN & LEMON ZEST

Normally I would make this recipe with seafood, like shrimp, but chicken creates a completely different flavour. SERVES 2

INGREDIENTS

- 1 lb (500 g) bow-tie pasta
- 2 Tbsp (30 mL) olive oil
- 1 carrot, julienned
- 2 cloves garlic, chopped
- 1 small red onion, chopped
- ½ cup (125 mL) sliced mushrooms
- 1 cup (250 mL) cooked chicken, cubed
- 1 cup (250 mL) chicken stock
- 2 Tbsp (30 mL) lemon juice
- 1 Tbsp (15 mL) lemon zest
- ½ tsp (2 mL) dried basil
- ½ tsp (2 mL) sea salt
- ½ tsp (2 mL) ground black pepper

METHOD

1. Bring a large pot of salted water to a boil. Cook the pasta for 8–10 minutes, or until *al dente*.

2. While the pasta is cooking, heat the oil in a small pot. Sauté the carrot, garlic, onion, and mushrooms for 2–3 minutes. Add all of the remaining ingredients. Cook for 5 minutes, stirring gently.

3. Drain the pasta and return to the pot. Add the sauce and mix well for 1–2 minutes. Serve immediately.

SHOPPING LIST

SPAGHETTI	$1.16
CARROT	$0.19
GARLIC	$0.07
RED ONION	$0.33
MUSHROOMS	$1.73
LEMON	$0.33
CHICKEN	$3.84
TOTAL	**$7.65**

BOW-TIE PASTA WITH SMOKED SALMON & CAPERS

This complete meal is tasty, healthy, and very easy to make. For a vegetarian (and even more economical) option, replace the salmon with 2 cups (500 mL) of sliced mushrooms. SERVES 2

INGREDIENTS

1 lb (500 g) bow-tie pasta

2 Tbsp (30 mL) olive oil

¾ cup (185 mL) smoked salmon, chopped

1 small onion, diced

2 cloves garlic, minced

¼ cup (60 mL) capers

½ cup (125 mL) light cream or whipping cream

½ tsp (2 mL) dried basil

½ tsp (2 mL) sea salt

½ tsp (2 mL) ground black pepper

METHOD

1. Bring a large pot of salted water to a boil. Cook the pasta for 7–10 minutes, or until *al dente*.

2. While the pasta is cooking, heat the oil in a large saucepan. Gently sauté the smoked salmon, onion, and garlic for 3–5 minutes. Add the capers and continue to sauté for 2 minutes more.

3. Add all of the remaining ingredients and allow to simmer for 4–5 minutes. Drain the pasta and return it to the pot. Fold it in the sauce, stirring gently. Serve immediately.

SHOPPING LIST

BOW-TIE PASTA	$0.99
SMOKED SALMON	$3.99
ONION	$0.13
GARLIC	$0.07
CAPERS	$2.28
TOTAL	**$7.46**

SHRIMP PENNE WITH FRESH PARSLEY & RED WINE

Shrimp is available fresh or frozen in just about any supermarket. I make this for dinner all the time. Cooked turkey or chicken works just as well. SERVES 2

INGREDIENTS

1 lb (500 g) penne

3 Tbsp (45 mL) olive oil

2 cloves garlic, chopped

1 small red onion, chopped

½ cup (125 mL) red cooking wine

½ cup (125 mL) vegetable stock

2 cups (500 mL) medium-sized shrimp, peeled and deveined

½ cup (125 mL) light cream or whipping cream

½ tsp (2 mL) dried basil

½ tsp (2 mL) dried thyme

½ tsp (2 mL) sea salt

½ tsp (2 mL) ground black pepper

½ cup (125 mL) grated Parmesan cheese

½ cup (125 mL) finely chopped fresh parsley or 2 Tbsp (30 mL) dried parsley

METHOD

1. Bring a large pot of salted water to a boil. Cook the pasta for 8–10 minutes, or until *al dente*.

2. While the pasta is cooking, heat the oil in a small pot. Sauté the garlic and onion for 2 minutes. Add the red wine. Cook for 2 minutes. Add all of the remaining ingredients, except the Parmesan cheese and parsley, and mix.

3. Drain the pasta and return it to the pot. Add the sauce and toss to coat. Top with the cheese and parsley and serve immediately.

SHOPPING LIST

PENNE	$1.22
GARLIC	$0.07
RED ONION	$0.33
SHRIMP	$3.59
PARMESAN CHEESE	$2.59
FRESH PARSLEY	$0.99
TOTAL	$8.79

PAD THAI WITH SEAFOOD, LEMON & FRESH CORIANDER

Mixed seafood is easy to find in the frozen food section of your supermarket.
It usually comes as a combination of shrimp, clams, squid, octopus, cuttlefish, and mussels
in packages of about ⅔ lb (350 g) and for under $5.00. This combination of vegetables
goes just as well with cooked chicken or pork. SERVES 2

INGREDIENTS

1 lb (500 g) dried rice noodles

3 Tbsp (45 mL) olive oil

2 cloves garlic, chopped

2 carrots, julienned

1 small red onion, chopped

½ cup (125 mL) snow peas, sliced

2 cups (500 mL) mixed seafood

½ cup (125 mL) soy sauce

¼ cup (60 mL) vegetable stock

3 Tbsp (45 mL) liquid honey

2 Tbsp (30 mL) lemon juice

1 Tbsp (15 mL) lemon zest

½ tsp (2 mL) dried basil

¼ tsp (1 mL) red pepper flakes

3 green onions, sliced

½ cup (125 mL) chopped fresh coriander

METHOD

1. Place the rice noodles in a large bowl. Cover with hot water. Let stand until the noodles soften, about 30 minutes, and drain well.

2. Heat the oil in a large saucepan. Sauté the garlic, carrots, onion, and snow peas for 2–3 minutes. Add all of the remaining ingredients, except the green onions and coriander. Cook for 5 minutes, stirring gently.

3. Add the drained noodles and mix well for 1–2 minutes to heat through. Top with green onions and chopped coriander. Serve immediately.

SHOPPING LIST

RICE NOODLES	$1.99
GARLIC	$0.07
CARROTS	$0.38
RED ONION	$0.33
SNOW PEAS	$1.49
MIXED SEAFOOD	$2.99
LEMON	$0.33
GREEN ONIONS	$0.62
FRESH CORIANDER	$0.94
TOTAL	$9.14

RIGATONI WITH BLUE CHEESE, SPINACH & HERBS

This pasta dish is very rich in flavour but uses simple ingredients like spinach, herbs, and blue cheese (such as Stilton, Gorgonzola, or Roquefort). You can serve it as a main meal for two or as an appetizer for four. SERVES 2

INGREDIENTS

- 1 lb (500 g) rigatoni
- 2 Tbsp (30 mL) olive oil
- 1 small red bell pepper, chopped
- 1 small red onion, chopped
- 2 cups (500 mL) chopped spinach
- 1 cup (250 mL) vegetable stock
- ½ cup (125 mL) light cream or whipping cream
- ¼ cup (60 mL) cubed or crumbled blue cheese
- ½ tsp (2 mL) dried basil
- ½ tsp (2 mL) dried oregano
- ½ tsp (2 mL) dried thyme
- ½ tsp (2 mL) sea salt
- ½ tsp (2 mL) ground black pepper
- ¼ cup (60 mL) chopped fresh parsley

METHOD

1. Bring a large pot of salted water to a boil. Cook the pasta for 8–10 minutes, or until *al dente.*

2. While the pasta is cooking, heat the oil in a large saucepan. Sauté the red bell pepper and red onion for 2 minutes and then add all of the remaining ingredients, except the parsley. Simmer the sauce for about 10 minutes, or until it thickens.

3. Drain the pasta and return to the pot. Add the sauce and toss to coat. Sprinkle the parsley on top. Serve immediately.

SHOPPING LIST

RIGATONI	$1.22
RED BELL PEPPER	$0.96
RED ONION	$0.33
SPINACH	$1.98
BLUE CHEESE	$3.39
FRESH PARSLEY	$0.99
TOTAL	**$8.87**

FUSILLI WITH PROSCIUTTO & LEEKS

Leeks are related to both garlic and onions but have a milder, subtler flavour and require a longer cooking time. You can replace the leeks with 3 cups (750 mL) of chopped spinach. SERVES 2

INGREDIENTS

1 lb (500 g) fusilli

2 Tbsp (30 mL) olive oil

1 carrot, chopped

1 celery stalk, chopped

1 small onion, chopped

2 cloves garlic, chopped

12–14 prosciutto slices, cut into ½-inch (1 cm) pieces

1 leek, cleaned and cut lengthwise into thin slices

2 cups (500 mL) vegetable stock

2 Tbsp (30 mL) balsamic vinegar

½ tsp (2 mL) dried basil

½ tsp (2 mL) dried oregano

½ tsp (2 mL) dried thyme

½ tsp (2 mL) sea salt

½ tsp (2 mL) ground black pepper

½ cup (125 mL) chopped fresh Italian parsley

¼ cup (60 mL) grated Parmesan cheese

METHOD

1. Bring a large pot of salted water to a boil. Cook the pasta for 8–10 minutes, or until *al dente*.

2. While the pasta is cooking, heat the oil in a large saucepan. Sauté the carrot, celery, onion, and garlic for about 2 minutes. Add the prosciutto. Cook for 3–4 minutes. Add all of the remaining ingredients, except the parsley and Parmesan cheese. Bring to a boil then reduce the heat. Simmer the sauce for 10–12 minutes, or until the liquid is reduced by half.

3. Drain the pasta and return it to the pot. Add the sauce and toss to coat. Add the parsley and Parmesan cheese. Toss. Serve immediately.

SHOPPING LIST

FUSILLI	$1.09
CARROT	$0.19
CELERY	$1.67
ONION	$0.13
GARLIC	$0.07
PROSCIUTTO	$2.89
LEEK	$0.76
FRESH ITALIAN PARSLEY	$0.99
PARMESAN CHEESE	$1.30
TOTAL	$9.09

RICE & GRAINS

MUSHROOM RISOTTO WITH PARMESAN & HERBS

Risotto isn't as hard to make as you may think, if you use my method below. This simple recipe gives restaurant quality for a fraction of the cost. SERVES 2

INGREDIENTS

2 Tbsp (30 mL) olive oil

1 small onion, chopped

2 cloves garlic, chopped

2 cups (500 mL) mushrooms, sliced

½ tsp (2 mL) dried thyme

½ tsp (2 mL) dried basil

1½ cups (375 mL) arborio rice (uncooked)

4 cups (1 L) chicken stock

½ cup (125 mL) grated Parmesan cheese

METHOD

1. Heat the oil in a large saucepan. Sauté the onion, garlic, and mushrooms for 4–5 minutes.

2. Add the thyme, basil, arborio rice, and chicken stock. Bring to a boil then reduce the heat. Simmer, stirring occasionally, for about 20 minutes, or until the rice has absorbed the stock.

3. Add the grated Parmesan and mix until smooth. Serve immediately.

SHOPPING LIST

ONION	$0.13
GARLIC	$0.07
MUSHROOMS	$1.73
ARBORIO RICE	$3.03
PARMESAN CHEESE	$2.59
TOTAL	$7.55

EASY PAELLA WITH RED WINE & SAFFRON

There are different versions of this incredible rice dish, which originated in Spain. This is one of my favourites. You can replace the chicken with cooked turkey or pork and use scallops instead of shrimp. SERVES 2

INGREDIENTS

3 Tbsp (45 mL) olive oil

1 celery stalk, chopped

1 green bell pepper, chopped

1 small onion, chopped

¼ tsp (1 mL) saffron threads

4 cups (1 L) chicken stock

1½ cups (375 mL) short-grain rice (uncooked)

1 mild chorizo sausage, sliced

½ cup (125 mL) red cooking wine

½ tsp (2 mL) dried basil

½ tsp (2 mL) dried oregano

½ tsp (2 mL) dried rosemary

½ tsp (2 mL) hot pepper flakes

1 cup (250 mL) shrimp, peeled and deveined

½ cup (125 mL) cooked, cubed chicken or turkey

¼ cup (60 mL) chopped fresh parsley

METHOD

1. Heat the oil in a wok or large sauté pan. Sauté the celery, green bell pepper, and onion for 3–4 minutes. Place the saffron threads in ¼ cup (60 mL) of boiling water and let sit for 15 minutes.

2. Add all of the remaining ingredients, except the shrimp, chicken, and parsley. Bring to a boil then reduce the heat. Add the saffron water and simmer for 10 minutes. Add the shrimp and chicken for another 5 minutes, or until the rice has absorbed the stock. If the rice becomes too dry, add more stock before it is cooked through.

3. Add the fresh parsley and serve.

SHOPPING LIST

CELERY	$1.29
GREEN BELL PEPPER	$0.49
ONION	$0.13
RICE	$0.96
SHRIMP	$2.24
CHICKEN	$1.51
CHORIZO SAUSAGE	$0.60
FRESH PARSLEY	$0.99
TOTAL	$8.21

KENNY'S SECRET FRIED RICE WITH BACON & FRESH CORIANDER

My mother made the best fried rice. One day she finally told me that it was the bacon that gave the dish its incredible flavour. SERVES 2

INGREDIENTS

1 tsp (5 mL) olive oil

2 eggs, beaten

¼ lb (125 g) bacon, chopped

2 cloves garlic, chopped

1 red bell pepper, chopped

1 small onion, chopped

1 cup (250 mL) mushrooms, sliced

1½ cups (375 mL) cooked white rice

½ cup (125 mL) soy sauce

½ tsp (2 mL) chopped fresh ginger

½ tsp (2 mL) dried basil

¼ cup (60 mL) chopped fresh coriander (or parsley)

METHOD

1. Heat the oil in a large sauté pan or wok and scramble the eggs. Remove the scrambled eggs and set aside. Cook the bacon in the same pan for 3–5 minutes.

2. Add the garlic, red bell pepper, onion, mushrooms, and rice. Sauté, mixing, for 4–6 minutes.

3. Add all of the remaining ingredients, except the coriander and scrambled eggs. Continue to sauté and mix for another 3–5 minutes. Add the chopped coriander and scrambled egg and serve.

SHOPPING LIST

BACON	$2.82
GARLIC	$0.07
RED BELL PEPPER	$1.56
ONION	$0.13
MUSHROOMS	$1.73
WHITE RICE	$0.96
FRESH GINGER	$0.25
FRESH CORIANDER	$0.94
TOTAL	$8.46

CHICKEN GUMBO WITH WHITE WINE & SUN-DRIED TOMATOES

If you like rice, this chicken gumbo is going to be a real treat. It has all the elements of New Orleans and the south. You can also use ground turkey or beef. SERVES 2

INGREDIENTS

- 2 Tbsp (30 mL) olive oil
- 1 lb (500 g) lean ground chicken
- 2 celery stalks, chopped
- 1 green bell pepper, chopped
- 1 red onion, chopped
- 2 cups (500 mL) chicken stock
- one 14 oz (398 mL) can diced tomatoes
- ½ cup (125 mL) finely chopped sun-dried tomatoes
- ½ cup (125 mL) white cooking wine
- 1 tsp (5 mL) dried thyme
- ½ tsp (2 mL) sea salt
- ½ tsp (2 mL) ground black pepper
- ¼ tsp (1 mL) red pepper flakes
- 1 cup (250 mL) long-grain rice (uncooked)

METHOD

1. Heat 1 Tbsp (15 mL) of the oil in a saucepan. Sauté the ground chicken for 8–10 minutes, or until browned. Remove from the pan and set aside. Add the remaining oil and sauté the celery, green bell pepper, and onion for 2–3 minutes.
2. Add all of the remaining ingredients, except the rice. Bring to a boil. Add the rice. Cook, covered, for 10–12 minutes.
3. Return the chicken to the pan. Simmer for 3–5 minutes, or until the rice is cooked. Serve immediately.

SHOPPING LIST

GROUND CHICKEN	$2.99
CELERY	$1.67
GREEN BELL PEPPER	$0.76
RED ONION	$0.40
CANNED TOMATOES	$0.87
SUN-DRIED TOMATOES	$1.35
LONG-GRAIN RICE	$0.45
TOTAL	**$8.49**

WHITE BEANS & RICE WITH SAUSAGE & FRESH CORIANDER

Beans, beans, beans; I love them. This South American dish uses white beans and sausage but you can use your favourite beans and chicken or turkey. SERVES 2

INGREDIENTS

2 Tbsp (30 mL) olive oil

2 cloves garlic, chopped

1 celery stalk, chopped

1 small green bell pepper, chopped

1 small red onion, chopped

2 cups (500 mL) vegetable stock

½ cup (125 mL) mild salsa

1 tsp (5 mL) chili powder

½ tsp (2 mL) dried basil

½ tsp (2 mL) sea salt

½ cup (125 mL) cooked or canned white kidney beans

2 chorizo sausages, cooked and sliced

1 cup (250 mL) of your favourite rice (uncooked)

¼ cup (60 mL) fresh coriander (or parsley)

METHOD

1. Heat the oil in a saucepan. Sauté the garlic, celery, green bell pepper, and onion for 2–3 minutes.

2. Add the vegetable stock, salsa, chili powder, basil, and salt. Bring to a boil then reduce the heat. Add the kidney beans, sausage, and rice. Simmer, covered, for 10–15 minutes, or until the rice is cooked.

3. Mix in the coriander. Serve immediately.

SHOPPING LIST

GARLIC	$0.07
CELERY	$1.67
GREEN BELL PEPPER	$0.51
RED ONION	$0.33
SALSA	$2.99
WHITE KIDNEY BEANS	$0.78
CHORIZO SAUSAGE	$1.20
RICE	$0.45
FRESH CORIANDER	$0.94
TOTAL	$8.94

JAMBALAYA WITH CHORIZO & MUSSELS

The one constant in jambalaya is rice. After that, anything goes. It's always a symphony of flavours.

SERVES 2

INGREDIENTS

3 Tbsp (45 mL) olive oil

1 red onion, chopped

2 celery stalks, chopped

1 small green bell pepper, chopped

2 cloves garlic, chopped

½ tsp (2 mL) cayenne pepper

¼ tsp (1 mL) saffron

1 cup (250 mL) cooked long-grain rice

one 14 oz (398 mL) can diced tomatoes, with juice

½ cup (125 mL) chopped green onions

3 cups (750 mL) chicken stock

8 mussels, debearded and scrubbed well to remove dirt

1 chorizo sausage, diced into ½-inch (1 cm) pieces

METHOD

1. Heat the oil in a saucepan or wok on medium heat. Add all of the ingredients, except the mussels and sausage, and combine well. Bring to a boil.
2. Gently mix in the mussels and chorizo.
3. Continue to cook until all the liquid has evaporated, 15–20 minutes. The mussels will have opened. Serve immediately.

SHOPPING LIST

RED ONION	$0.40
CELERY	$1.67
GREEN BELL PEPPER	$0.51
GARLIC	$0.07
LONG-GRAIN RICE	$0.45
CANNED TOMATOES	$0.87
GREEN ONIONS	$0.49
MUSSELS	$4.49
CHORIZO SAUSAGE	$0.60
TOTAL	**$9.55**

COUSCOUS WITH ORANGE & DATES

I use dates to sweeten certain recipes with a natural flavour. They are a good source of protein and iron. Dried apricots and raisins work just as well. SERVES 2

INGREDIENTS

2 Tbsp (30 mL) olive oil

1 small red onion, chopped

2 cloves garlic, chopped

½ cup (125 mL) dates, pitted and chopped

½ cup (125 mL) vegetable stock

½ cup (125 mL) orange juice

2 Tbsp (30 mL) orange zest

2 Tbsp (30 mL) lemon juice

½ tsp (2 mL) dried basil

½ tsp (2 mL) dried thyme

½ tsp (2 mL) sea salt

½ tsp (2 mL) ground black pepper

1 cup (250 mL) uncooked couscous

¼ cup (60 mL) chopped fresh parsley

yellow bell pepper, chopped (optional)

METHOD

1. Heat the oil in a medium-sized saucepan. Sauté the onion and garlic for 2 minutes. Add all of the remaining ingredients, except the couscous and parsley. Bring to a boil then reduce to a simmer.

2. Add all of the couscous. Cover, and remove the pot from the heat. Let stand for 10 minutes, or until the couscous has absorbed the liquid.

3. Mix in the parsley. Top with chopped yellow pepper, if using. Serve immediately.

SHOPPING LIST

RED ONION	$0.33
GARLIC	$0.07
DATES	$1.79
ORANGE	$1.03
LEMON	$0.33
COUSCOUS	$1.89
FRESH PARSLEY	$0.99
TOTAL	$6.43

LAMB & COUSCOUS WITH ROSEMARY, OLIVES & FETA

Couscous makes a great main meal because it's quick and easy. Combined with lamb, fresh rosemary, and olives, it offers a dish with healthy European flavour. If you don't like lamb, you can use beef or cubed chicken. SERVES 2

INGREDIENTS

2 Tbsp (30 mL) olive oil

1 lb (500 g) stewing lamb, cubed

1 small red onion, chopped

2 cloves garlic, chopped

1 cup (250 mL) beef stock

½ cup (125 mL) olives, sliced

½ cup (125 mL) red cooking wine

1 tsp (5 mL) dried rosemary

1 cup (250 mL) uncooked couscous

½ cup (125 mL) crumbled feta cheese

METHOD

1. Heat the oil in a large saucepan. Brown the lamb for 5–8 minutes. Add the onion and garlic and sauté for 2–3 minutes more.

2. Add all of the remaining ingredients, except the couscous and feta cheese. Bring to a boil then reduce the heat. Simmer for another 3–5 minutes.

3. Add the couscous. Cover and remove the pan from the heat. Let stand for 10–15 minutes, or until the couscous has absorbed the liquid. Sprinkle the feta cheese on top. Serve immediately.

SHOPPING LIST

STEWING LAMB	$4.99
RED ONION	$0.31
GARLIC	$0.07
OLIVES	$1.69
COUSCOUS	$1.05
FETA CHEESE	$1.89
TOTAL	$10.00

MARINADES & DRESSINGS

CREAMY RED PEPPER DIJON SAUCE

This sauce is creamy and versatile.

MAKES 1½ CUPS (375 ML)

INGREDIENTS

1 cup (250 mL) chicken or vegetable stock

½ cup (125 mL) yogurt

1 red bell pepper, chopped

3 Tbsp (45 mL) Dijon mustard

2 Tbsp (30 mL) balsamic vinegar

¼ tsp (1 mL) dried basil

¼ tsp (1 mL) chili powder

METHOD

1. Bring the stock to a boil in a small saucepan, and immediately reduce the heat so that the stock is simmering. Add the yogurt, gently whisking it into the stock.
2. Add all of the remaining ingredients. Simmer the mixture over medium heat for about 5 minutes, stirring constantly.
3. Serve over pasta, rice, meats, fish, or poultry.

MUSHROOM & APPLE "CAVIAR"

Mushrooms and apples make inexpensive "caviar." I use button mushrooms, but you can use the mushrooms of your choice.

MAKES 3 CUPS (750 ML)

INGREDIENTS

2 cups (500 mL) chopped button mushrooms

1 small red onion, chopped

1 small apple, peeled, cored, and chopped

1 cup (250 mL) apple juice

1 cup (250 mL) vegetable stock

⅓ cup (80 mL) balsamic vinegar

½ tsp (2 mL) dried basil

½ tsp (2 mL) dried oregano

METHOD

1. Combine all of the ingredients in a small saucepan.
2. Cook the mixture on low heat for 8–10 minutes, or until the liquid is reduced by half.
3. Serve over pasta, rice, or grilled foods.

PEANUT SAUCE WITH COCONUT MILK

I love versatile sauces, like this peanut and coconut one. You can use regular dairy milk instead of the coconut milk. Either way, it's good with rice or noodles, or even on top of stir-fries. Add another cup of coconut milk to the recipe and you have a great marinade for meats and poultry.
MAKES 3 CUPS (750 ML)

INGREDIENTS

3 Tbsp (45 mL) olive oil

2 cloves garlic, chopped

1 small onion, chopped

1 small red bell pepper, chopped

1 cup (250 mL) coconut milk

1 cup (250 mL) vegetable stock

1 cup (250 mL) smooth peanut butter

METHOD

1. Heat the oil in a small saucepan. Sauté the garlic, onion, and red bell pepper for 2–3 minutes.

2. Add all of the remaining ingredients. Simmer the mixture on low heat for 5–6 minutes.

3. If the sauce is too thick, add more coconut milk or stock to thin it out.

QUICK TOMATO SAUCE WITH HERBS & GARLIC

Herbs and tomatoes always make a flavourful combination for pasta, rice, meats, fish, poultry, or vegetables. Here, I use basil and rosemary, but you can also use fresh coriander leaves and tarragon. Add 4 more cups (1 L) of stock and you have an inexpensive homemade tomato base for soup. MAKES
2½–3 CUPS (625–750 ML)

INGREDIENTS

3 Tbsp (45 mL) olive oil

2 cloves garlic, chopped

2 celery stalks, chopped

1 medium onion, chopped

one 28 oz (796 mL) can diced tomatoes

1 cup (250 mL) vegetable stock

½ cup (125 mL) kernel corn, canned or frozen

½ tsp (2 mL) dried basil

½ tsp (2 mL) dried rosemary

½ tsp (2 mL) sea salt

METHOD

1. Heat the oil in a medium-sized saucepan. Sauté the garlic, celery, and onion for 2–3 minutes, or until the onion is translucent.

2. Add all of the remaining ingredients and mix well. Simmer the mixture for 8–10 minutes.

3. Serve warm over pasta, rice, meats, fish, poultry, or vegetables.

TANGY RELISH WITH HONEY

- -

*Store-bought relish is expensive. This affordable
homemade relish can be served with almost anything.
If you want to splurge a bit, replace the onions
with 4 cups (1 L) of chopped mushrooms.*

MAKES 1½ CUPS (325 ML)

INGREDIENTS

3 Tbsp (45 mL) olive oil

3 medium onions, finely sliced

1 green bell pepper, diced

½ cup (125 mL) vegetable stock

½ cup (125 mL) apple juice

¼ cup (60 mL) liquid honey

2 Tbsp (30 mL) balsamic vinegar

½ tsp (2 mL) dried basil

½ tsp (2 mL) dried rosemary

¼ tsp (1 mL) ground black pepper

METHOD

1. Heat the oil in a small saucepan. Gently
   sauté the onions and green bell pepper
   for 2–3 minutes.
2. Add all of the remaining ingredients. Bring
   to a boil then reduce the heat. Simmer the
   mixture for 10–12 minutes, or until the
   liquid is reduced by half.
3. Serve the relish warm on pasta, rice, meats,
   fish, poultry, or vegetables.

APPLE & CINNAMON MARINADE

- -

*Apples and cinnamon aren't just for apple
pie. This marinade adds restaurant-quality taste
with everyday ingredients.*

MAKES 1 CUP (250 ML)

INGREDIENTS

½ cup (125 mL) olive oil

½ cup (125 mL) liquid honey

½ cup (125 mL) apple juice

¼ cup (60 mL) applesauce

¼ cup (60 mL) soy sauce

½ tsp (2 mL) cinnamon

METHOD

1. Combine all of the ingredients in a bowl
   and whisk until smooth.
2. Use as a marinade for meats, especially pork
   and lamb, and also with poultry and fish.
3. Reserve some marinade to brush on while
   baking or grilling.

CITRUS & GARLIC WITH SUN-DRIED TOMATO MARINADE

Here's another example of versatility. Mix in 1 cup (250 mL) of sour cream, and serve as a dip with skewers of meat or chicken, or for vegetables.

MAKES 1 CUP (250 ML)

INGREDIENTS

½ cup (125 mL) olive oil

½ cup (125 mL) orange juice

½ cup (125 mL) chopped sun-dried tomatoes

2 cloves garlic, finely chopped

2 Tbsp (30 mL) orange zest

2 Tbsp (30 mL) lemon juice

METHOD

1. Combine all of the ingredients in a bowl and whisk until smooth.

2. Use as a marinade, especially for poultry and fish.

3. Reserve some marinade to brush on while baking or grilling.

CREAMY HERB MARINADE

Mix ¼ cup (60 mL) of the marinade mixture with ¼ cup (60 mL) of olive oil and you have a salad dressing.

MAKES ¾ CUP (185 ML)

INGREDIENTS

½ cup (125 mL) vegetable stock

2 Tbsp (30 mL) balsamic vinegar

2 Tbsp (30 mL) Dijon mustard

1½ tsp (7.5 mL) sour cream

½ tsp (2 mL) dried basil

½ tsp (2 mL) dried thyme

½ tsp (2 mL) dried oregano

½ tsp (2 mL) sea salt

½ tsp (2 mL) ground black pepper

METHOD

1. Combine all of the ingredients in a bowl and whisk until smooth.

2. Use as a marinade for meats, poultry, fish, and vegetables.

3. Reserve some marinade to brush on while baking or grilling.

QUICK TERIYAKI & GINGER MARINADE

Rather than expensive store-bought teriyaki sauce, try this homemade version for cooking and grilling.

MAKES 1 CUP (250 ML)

INGREDIENTS

½ cup (125 mL) soy sauce

½ cup (125 mL) pineapple juice

2 Tbsp (30 mL) liquid honey

1 Tbsp (15 mL) sesame oil

1 Tbsp (15 mL) fresh minced ginger

METHOD

1. Combine all of the ingredients in a bowl and whisk until smooth.

2. Use as a marinade for meats, poultry, fish, vegetables, and firm tofu.

3. Reserve some marinade to brush on while baking or grilling.

TOMATO BARBECUE MARINADE

Here's another one of those versatile recipes. Add ¼ cup (60 mL) of olive oil and 2 Tbsp (30 mL) of balsamic vinegar to the recipe and you have a great homemade salad dressing.

MAKES 1 CUP (250 ML)

INGREDIENTS

½ cup (125 mL) mild or hot salsa

½ cup (125 mL) sour cream

¼ cup (60 mL) tomato juice

¼ cup (60 mL) olive oil

2 Tbsp (30 mL) Worcestershire sauce

1 tsp (5 mL) onion powder

1 tsp (5 mL) garlic powder

METHOD

1. Combine all of the ingredients in a bowl and whisk until smooth.

2. Use as a marinade for meats, poultry, or fish, and as a marinade or dip for vegetables.

3. Reserve some marinade to brush on while baking or grilling.

BLUE CHEESE & SUN-DRIED TOMATO DRESSING

- -

Here's a restaurant-quality blue cheese dressing. Add ½ cup (125 mL) of stock or ¼ cup (60 mL) of sour cream to this recipe and it doubles as a creamy, flavour-filled marinade for meat or poultry.

MAKES 1 CUP (250 ML)

INGREDIENTS

½ cup (125 mL) olive oil

¼ cup (60 mL) red wine vinegar

¼ cup (60 mL) crumbled blue cheese

¼ cup (60 mL) chopped sun-dried tomatoes

2 Tbsp (30 mL) balsamic vinegar

2 Tbsp (30 mL) sour cream

½ tsp (2 mL) sea salt

½ tsp (2 mL) ground black pepper

METHOD

1. Combine all of the ingredients in a bowl and whisk until smooth.

2. Serve over salad or any type of grilled food.

THE BEST CAESAR SALAD DRESSING

- -

This is the best Caesar dressing. It's also great as a grilling sauce for meats, poultry, fish, or vegetables AND it uses the items in your "essential" pantry (see page xi).

MAKES ⅔ CUP (160 ML)

INGREDIENTS

½ cup (125 mL) olive oil

¼ cup (60 mL) red wine vinegar

6 cloves garlic, finely chopped

2 Tbsp (30 mL) sour cream

1 Tbsp (15 mL) liquid honey

1 tsp (5 mL) Dijon mustard

1 tsp (5 mL) chili powder

½ tsp (2 mL) sea salt

½ tsp (2 mL) ground black pepper

METHOD

1. Combine all of the ingredients in a bowl and whisk until smooth.

2. Serve over romaine lettuce.

SWEET RED PEPPER & GARLIC DRESSING

----

*Red peppers and garlic make for a simple,
inexpensive homemade dressing, marinade,
or even stock. For a creamier dressing, add 1 Tbsp
(15 mL) of sour cream to the recipe. Add 1 cup
(250 mL) of apple juice and you have a marinade
for meats, poultry, fish, or vegetables.
Add 4 cups (1 L) of stock and it's a soup.
This one might win the versatility contest.*

MAKES 1 CUP (250 ML)

INGREDIENTS

½ red bell pepper, chopped

2 cloves garlic, chopped

½ cup (125 mL) olive oil

¼ cup (60 mL) red wine vinegar

2 Tbsp (30 mL) balsamic vinegar

½ tsp (2 mL) dried basil

½ tsp (2 mL) sea salt

½ tsp (2 mL) ground black pepper

METHOD

1. Combine all of the ingredients in a bowl
   and purée with a hand blender until smooth.
2. Serve over any salad.

CREAMY SESAME GARLIC DRESSING WITH GINGER

----

*This dressing is as good over grilled food
as it is over salad.*

MAKES 1 CUP (250 ML)

INGREDIENTS

2 cloves garlic, chopped

1 tsp (5 mL) freshly grated ginger

¼ cup (60 mL) sesame oil

¼ cup (60 mL) olive oil

¼ cup (60 mL) red wine vinegar

¼ cup (60 mL) sour cream

METHOD

1. Combine all of the ingredients in a bowl
   and whisk until smooth.
2. Serve over a salad or any type of grilled
   food.

STRAWBERRY & MINT DRESSING

- -

*This one has it all: it has flavour, it's easy to make,
it's economical, and it's versatile. Add 1 cup
(250 mL) of plain yogurt and it's a marinade.
Add ½ cup (125 mL) of sour cream and it's a dip.*

MAKES 1 CUP (250 ML)

INGREDIENTS

½ cup (125 mL) strawberry yogurt

¼ cup (60 mL) strawberries, finely chopped

¼ cup (60 mL) olive oil

2 Tbsp (30 mL) liquid honey

1 Tbsp (15 mL) red wine vinegar

½ tsp (2 mL) dried mint

METHOD

1. Combine all of the ingredients in a bowl and whisk until smooth.
2. Serve over a salad or any type of grilled food.

3 DINNERS
FOR 6
FOR UNDER $30

Mashed Potato Soup with Roasted Garlic
Steak & Lobster Penne with White Wine
The Best Caesar Salad
Grilled Apples with Brown Sugar

MASHED POTATO SOUP WITH ROASTED GARLIC

SERVES 6

INGREDIENTS

6 cups (1.5 L) vegetable stock

3 cups (750 mL) mashed potatoes

1 small onion, chopped

8 cloves garlic, roasted and chopped

2 Tbsp (30 mL) Dijon mustard

2 Tbsp (30 mL) balsamic vinegar

½ tsp (2 mL) dried basil

½ tsp (2 mL) dried oregano

½ tsp (2 mL) sea salt

½ tsp (2 mL) ground black pepper

1 cup (250 mL) light cream or whipping cream

2 Tbsp (30 mL) dried parsley

METHOD

1. Combine all of the ingredients, except the cream and parsley, in a large soup pot. Bring to a boil then reduce the heat. Simmer for about 15 minutes, stirring occasionally.

2. Add the cream. Simmer the soup for another 2–3 minutes.

3. Serve immediately, sprinkled with the parsley.

SHOPPING LIST

POTATOES	$2.16
ONION	$0.13
GARLIC	$0.07
TOTAL	$2.36

STEAK & LOBSTER PENNE WITH WHITE WINE

SERVES 6

INGREDIENTS

1 lb (500 g) penne

3 Tbsp (45 mL) olive oil

3 strip loin steaks, cut into strips

1 small onion, chopped

4 small rock lobster tails, peeled and sliced

1 cup (250 mL) white cooking wine

½ cup (125 mL) light cream or whipping cream

¼ cup (60 mL) balsamic vinegar

2 Tbsp (30 mL) Dijon mustard

1 tsp (5 mL) dried basil

1 tsp (5 mL) dried thyme

½ tsp (2 mL) sea salt

½ tsp (2 mL) ground black pepper

2 Tbsp (30 mL) dried parsley

METHOD

1. Bring a large pot of salted water to a boil. Cook the pasta for 8–10 minutes, or until *al dente*.

2. While the pasta is cooking, heat the oil in a large saucepan. Sauté the strip loin strips for 3–4 minutes. Add the onion and continue sautéing for another 2 minutes. Add all of the remaining ingredients, except the parsley. Simmer the sauce for about 5 minutes, or until it thickens.

3. Drain the pasta and return it to the pot. Add the sauce to the pasta and toss to coat. Sprinkle the parsley on top. Serve.

SHOPPING LIST

PENNE	$2.17
STRIP LOIN STEAK	$8.79
ONION	$0.13
LOBSTER TAILS	$8.99
TOTAL	$20.08

THE BEST CAESAR SALAD

SERVES 6

INGREDIENTS

3 romaine lettuce hearts
¾ cup (185 mL) The Best Caesar Salad
   Dressing (see page 153)

METHOD

1. Separate the leaves of the 3 romaine hearts
   into a large mixing bowl. Add the dressing
   and mix well.
2. Evenly distribute the salad onto 6 salad
   plates.

GRILLED APPLES WITH BROWN SUGAR

SERVE 6

INGREDIENTS

3 apples, peeled, cored, and cut into quarters
¼ cup (60 mL) brown sugar

METHOD

1. Grill the apple pieces on high heat, using
   an indoor or outdoor grill until you get nice
   grill marks. Remove from the grill.
2. Sprinkle the apple with the brown sugar and
   allow the heat to caramelize the sugar.
3. Serve warm.

SHOPPING LIST

ROMAINE HEARTS	$2.49
TOTAL	$2.49

SHOPPING LIST

APPLES	$1.77
TOTAL	$1.77

Cream of Zucchini Soup with Basil
Curry Fennel Salad with Sesame & Balsamic
Stuffed Pork Tenderloin
with Artichoke & Asparagus
Steamed Baby Carrots with Butter & Mint
Poached Pears with Cinnamon

CREAM OF ZUCCHINI SOUP WITH BASIL

SERVES 6

INGREDIENTS

2 Tbsp (30 mL) olive oil

1 small onion, chopped

2 cloves garlic, chopped

6 medium zucchini, chopped

6 cups (1.5 L) vegetable stock

½ tsp (2 mL) dried basil

½ tsp (2 mL) chili powder

½ tsp (2 mL) sea salt

½ tsp (2 mL) ground black pepper

½ cup (125 mL) light cream
   or whipping cream

METHOD

1. Heat the oil in a large pot and sauté the onion and garlic for 2–3 minutes. Add the zucchini and continue to sauté for another 5 minutes.

2. Add all of the remaining ingredients, except the cream. Bring to a boil then reduce the heat. Simmer for 10 minutes.

3. Using a hand blender, purée the soup until smooth. Add the cream and serve.

SHOPPING LIST

ONION	$0.13
GARLIC	$0.07
ZUCCHINI	$3.18
TOTAL	$3.38

CURRY FENNEL SALAD WITH SESAME & BALSAMIC

SERVES 6

INGREDIENTS

2 fennel bulbs

¼ cup (60 mL) balsamic vinegar

2 Tbsp (30 mL) olive oil

1 Tbsp (15 mL) sesame oil

½ tsp (2 mL) mild curry powder

¼ tsp (1 mL) dried tarragon

¼ tsp (1 mL) sea salt

¼ tsp (1 mL) ground pepper

METHOD

1. Remove the stalks and outside layer of the fennel, as well as the core. Shave the fennel into thin slices and place evenly on 6 plates.
2. Combine all of the remaining ingredients in a small mixing bowl and whisk until smooth.
3. Drizzle evenly over the 6 individual salads.

STUFFED PORK TENDER-LOIN WITH ARTICHOKE & ASPARAGUS

SERVES 6

INGREDIENTS

1 bunch asparagus, ends removed and chopped

1 cup (250 mL) marinated artichokes, chopped

3 cloves garlic, chopped

2 Tbsp (30 mL) Dijon mustard

2 Tbsp (30 mL) Worcestershire sauce

½ tsp (2 mL) dried thyme

2 Tbsp (30 mL) olive oil

½ tsp (2 mL) sea salt

½ tsp (2 mL) ground black pepper

2 large pork tenderloins, butterflied

½ tsp (2 mL) dried rosemary

METHOD

1. Combine everything, except the tenderloins and rosemary, in a large bowl. Mix well.
2. Place the mixture in the middle of the 2 pork tenderloins and gently fold each over. Sprinkle on the dried rosemary.
3. Place in a baking dish. Bake in a preheated oven at 350°F (180°C) for 20–25 minutes, or until tender. Cut evenly in 6 pieces.

SHOPPING LIST

FENNEL BULBS	$3.80
TOTAL	$3.80

SHOPPING LIST

ASPARAGUS	$2.99
ARTICHOKES	$1.49
GARLIC	$0.07
PORK TENDERLOIN	$11.72
TOTAL	$16.27

STEAMED BABY CARROTS WITH BUTTER & MINT

SERVES 6

INGREDIENTS

- 2 cups (500 mL) baby carrots, cleaned
- 2 Tbsp (30 mL) Dijon mustard
- 2 Tbsp (30 mL) butter
- ½ tsp (2 mL) dried mint
- ½ tsp (2 mL) sea salt
- ½ tsp (2 mL) ground black pepper

METHOD

1. Combine all of the ingredients in a large bowl. Mix well.
2. Using foil wrap, place everything in a foil pouch and close.
3. Bake in a preheated oven at 350°F (180°C) for 12–15 minutes, or until the carrots are tender.

POACHED PEARS WITH CINNAMON

SERVES 6

INGREDIENTS

- 3 cups (750 mL) water
- 3 Tbsp (45 mL) brown sugar (for poaching liquid)
- 1 tsp (5 mL) cinnamon
- 3 pears, cut in half
- 1 tsp (5 mL) brown sugar (for sprinkling)

METHOD

1. Combine the water, 3 Tbsp (45 mL) brown sugar, and cinnamon in a large saucepan. Bring to a boil then reduce the heat.
2. Place the pears in the mixture and allow them to simmer for 4–5 minutes. Turn once and simmer for another 2–4 minutes.
3. Remove the pears and cool in the refrigerator for at least an hour prior to serving. Plate the pear halves. Sprinkle with the remaining brown sugar and serve.

```
SHOPPING LIST
--------------------
BABY CARROTS         $1.29
_____
TOTAL                $1.29
```

```
SHOPPING LIST
--------------------
PEARS                $2.07
_____
TOTAL                $2.07
```

Vegetable End Soup
Chickpea & Herb Salad
Roasted Quail with Rosemary
Garlic Roasted Potatoes with Mint
Diced Zucchini with Onion & Herbs

VEGETABLE END SOUP

SERVES 6

INGREDIENTS

6 cups (1.5 L) vegetable stock

4 cups (1 L) mixed vegetables (or leftover vegetables)

1 small onion, chopped

2 cloves garlic, chopped

2 Tbsp (30 mL) balsamic vinegar

1 Tbsp (15 mL) Dijon mustard

½ tsp (2 mL) dried basil

½ tsp (2 mL) dried oregano

½ tsp (2 mL) dried thyme

½ tsp (2 mL) sea salt

½ tsp (2 mL) ground black pepper

METHOD

1. Combine all of the ingredients in a large pot. Bring to a boil.

2. Reduce the heat and simmer for 20 minutes.

3. Using a hand blender, purée the soup until smooth.

SHOPPING LIST

MIXED VEGETABLES	$2.99
ONION	$0.13
GARLIC	$0.07
TOTAL	$3.19

CHICKPEA & HERB SALAD

SERVES 6

INGREDIENTS

2 cups (500 mL) chickpeas

1 large tomato, chopped

1 small onion, chopped

½ cup (125 mL) olive oil

¼ cup (60 mL) red wine vinegar

1 Tbsp (15 mL) sugar

1 tsp (5 mL) chili powder

½ tsp (2 mL) dried basil

½ tsp (2 mL) dried thyme

½ tsp (2 mL) sea salt

½ tsp (2 mL) ground black pepper

METHOD

1. Combine all of the ingredients in a bowl and mix well.
2. Let sit in the refrigerator for at least 30 minutes before serving.
3. Mix again before serving.

ROASTED QUAIL WITH ROSEMARY

SERVES 6

INGREDIENTS

½ cup (125 mL) olive oil

6 quail

1 Tbsp (15 mL) dried rosemary

½ tsp (2 mL) sea salt

½ tsp (2 mL) ground black pepper

METHOD

1. Brush olive oil on each quail. Sprinkle each with rosemary, sea salt, and pepper.
2. Place the quail in a baking pan. Bake in a preheated oven at 350°F (180°C) for 20–25 minutes.
3. Let sit for 5 minutes prior to serving.

```
SHOPPING LIST
--------------------
CHICKPEAS          $0.81
TOMATO             $0.88
ONION              $0.13
--------------------
TOTAL              $1.82
```

```
SHOPPING LIST
--------------------
QUAIL             $19.99
--------------------
TOTAL             $19.99
```

GARLIC ROASTED POTATOES WITH MINT

SERVES 6

INGREDIENTS

5 medium potatoes, peeled and cubed
½ cup (125 mL) olive oil
1 tsp (5 mL) garlic powder
1 tsp (5 mL) dried mint
½ tsp (2 mL) sea salt
½ tsp (2 mL) ground black pepper

METHOD

1. Place the potato cubes on a rimmed, non-stick baking pan.
2. Combine the garlic powder, mint, sea salt, and pepper in a bowl. Mix and sprinkle evenly over the potatoes.
3. Bake in a preheated oven at 350°F (180°C) for 20–25 minutes, or until golden.

DICED ZUCCHINI WITH ONION & HERBS

SERVES 6

INGREDIENTS

3 Tbsp (45 mL) olive oil
1 small onion, chopped
2 zucchini, diced
½ tsp (2 mL) dried basil
½ tsp (2 mL) dried thyme
½ tsp (2 mL) sea salt
½ tsp (2 mL) ground black pepper

METHOD

1. Heat the oil in a medium saucepan. Add the onion and sauté for about 3–4 minutes, or until translucent.
2. Add all of the remaining ingredients and sauté for 8–10 minutes, or until the zucchini is fully cooked.

```
     SHOPPING LIST
     ----------------

POTATOES            $1.80
_____
TOTAL               $1.80
```

```
     SHOPPING LIST
     ----------------

ONION               $0.13
ZUCCHINI            $1.06
_____
TOTAL               $1.19
```

ACKNOWLEDGEMENTS

The $10 Gourmet was an exciting challenge that I could not have completed on my own. There are several people who extended sound advice and continued support, and who were instrumental in the preparation of this book. Without them this book would have not materialized. To this great group—thank you!

—Ken

Desi Cabrera
Tanya Scata
Gill Humphreys
Mary Jo Eustace
Christy Burton
Craig Forrest
Nicole de Montbrun
Susan Fluellon
Robert McCullough
Michelle Mayne
Mauve Pagé
Melva McLean

Grace Yaginuma
Taryn Boyd
Lesley Cameron
Amanda LeNeve
Jennifer Goos
Bobb Barratt
Trevor Shaw
Napoleon
Josephine
Hercules
Kasper

INDEX